Secret Suicide

Secret Suicide

Donna Vella

Secret Suicide

© Donna Vella 2018

All rights reserved. Without limiting the rights under copyright reserved above, no part of this publication may be reproduced, stored in a retrieval system, or transmitted, in any form or by any means (electronic, mechanical, photocopying, recording or otherwise), without the prior written permission of the copyright owner of this book.

Published by
Lighthouse Christian Publishing
SAN 257-4330
5531 Dufferin Drive
Savage, Minnesota, 55378
United States of America

www.lighthousechristianpublishing.com

To Mom, Dad and Sis: There are no words to properly thank you.

Table of Contents

Introduction

Chapter 1   The Week Prior

Chapter 2   The Closet

Chapter 3   The Lie

Chapter 4   His Family

Chapter 5   Why?

Chapter 6   Suicide Victim

Chapter 7   Small Acts of Revenge

Chapter 8   Putting the Puzzle Together

Chapter 9   Other Stories

Chapter 10   The Ripple Effect

Chapter 11   Dating, working & alcohol

Chapter 12   Healing

Chapter 13   My Plea

Introduction

Hi. My name is Donna and this is my story. Let me first introduce myself. I became a widow at the age of forty-three with three young daughters ages eight, ten and twelve. One rainy summer Saturday afternoon while my kids were home watching a movie and I was drinking a cup of Starbucks coffee on our patio, my husband, with no warning whatsoever, committed suicide.

This book takes you through my journey. I have been lying to almost everyone. With the exception of my parents, my sister, one neighbor, my insurance guy, and the paramedics and police officers that assisted that awful day, nobody else knows the truth. No one would even believe the truth.

I've lied to you to already. My name isn't Donna. All of the names and some places have been changed to protect the innocent (my children) and the guilty (everyone else). So if I am so concerned with protecting my secret, why am I writing this book? Well, to my knowledge, none of my family or friends would have a reason to read this book. I do not think I am at much risk of "being outed". According to my therapist…and I spend a lot of time in therapy, documenting my thoughts, feelings and experiences is good for my healing process. So thank you in advance for being by my side during my healing time, through reading this book. I looked for books on suicide and survivors of suicide and I was not able to find a book that fit my situation. I feel like I am alone. The statistics of adult men committing suicide is higher than it has ever been and on the rise. Yet, you do not hear of it that often…which makes me think that I am not the only wife out there living a lie with the goal of protecting the children and our husbands' legacies. If you are a suicide survivor living a lie, know that you are not alone. I understand why you lie. It's ok to be angry but you also need to be grateful. We are survivors...don't ever forget it.

I am hoping I can save just one person. This is the only way I know how to help. Running a 5k or tattooing a semi-colon to my ass is not going to help anyone. I am sure that most people fantasize about suicide at least one time in their life. I know I wished I were dead when I found out that my husband was having a ten- month long love affair. But then there is the planning stage. Although suicide seems to be a spontaneous act, there is planning. People decide in advance how and where they are going to do it. The when is usually the spontaneous part. If you are in the fantasy or planning stage, please seek professional help and then keep reading. **All I ask is that you take a moment to step out of your own grief and pain, and put yourself in the shoes of your survivors.** My intention is not to be insincere or minimize your own internal struggle, **it is just to give you a flavor of the tragedy and all the people you will hurt for the rest of their lives in the wake of your suicide. You won't be here to see it, so I will show you now.** I sincerely hope you will change your mind. You intentionally hurting yourself will unintentionally hurt many others.

I am not a psychologist. Not even close. My background is in finance and accounting and I have been a stay-at-home mom for several years. My husband always said I had a talent in making what seemed to be a complicated situation, sensible and easy to understand. I know how to cut to the chase! If this weren't my life, I would have to agree that it is a pretty interesting story. It has it all... sex, lies, violence, and mystery. Besides names being changed, this story is 100% true and falls under the umbrella of "you can't make this shit up". I don't want you to feel sorry for me. I am living my life and taking care of my kids. I no longer have the happiness or the "perfect life" I once had but I will survive and I am grateful. If you are wondering if I am angry, the answer is yes, I am. I am really pissed. There is no happy ending. There is no knight in shining armor. I am still writing my own ending.

I would like to begin this book with an excerpt from a letter I wrote my daughters a couple of months after my husband died. The original letter is located in a safe deposit box with the long-form death certificates. There in black and white, an official government document stating, Cause of Death: *suicide*. I included copies of emails between us so that my daughters can see that we were trying to save our marriage. His emails spoke of future plans and growing old together. I hope if they ever find the death certificates that my letter and copies of old emails between us will answer some of my daughters' many questions and minimize their anger towards him and me.

Dear Girls, If you are reading this letter then you have come across your father's long form death certificate stating cause of death suicide. I hope you are reading this many years into the future (but hopefully never at all). Daddy has been gone for only three months and two days at the time I am writing this letter. I feel as though I should write everything down while it is still fresh, answer all of the questions I anticipate you having before memories change and get lost in time.

As you can see, his death was a suicide, not a heart attack. I did not lie to you when I told you daddy was very sick and we didn't know it. He was sick, mental illness, not a bad heart. Before you become furious and angry with me for lying to you, please take the time to read this letter. Let me plead my case for lying and let me try to answer the questions I know you have with the limited information I have. I know your questions are:

"Why did your father die by suicide", "Why did I cover it up" "Who knows the truth"

I don't know why. I will tell you what was going on in his life immediately prior to his death, but I can only speculate what haunted him in his past prior to even meeting me. You will learn some unpleasant truths about your father so stop reading if you would rather not know...

Chapter One: The Week Prior

I got the greatest thrill from seeing your reactions to our three-pack of pint-sized adventures. Your excitement about the flight tour was especially intoxicating to me. I invite you to many, many more fun (and maybe sometimes annoying) adventures big and small.
I promise it's just the beginning. My enthusiasm will not ever wane. I enjoy digging in and drawing you close to me, without apprehension.
You are an amazing woman. I feel beyond lucky and fortunate to be with you. I'll make sure you feel it forevermore, and that our lives will be richer for the journey.
I love you, now and forever. I'll jump every hurdle on the way to show you, and I'll never let anything in our future get in the way. (E-mail from my husband to myself four days prior to his death).

He died on a Saturday. The Monday evening prior, we decided to do something special together, just the two of us without the kids. In an effort to get our marriage back on track, we were both trying. Sometimes with and sometimes without the kids, we would try different restaurants and experiences. We chartered a small aircraft to take us up the coast. It was the smallest airplane I had ever flown in. We joked that the tiny airplane was a Volkswagen with wings. I was scared to death, but it turned out to be a very pleasant experience. We had fun. This wasn't unusual; we always had fun together and sincerely enjoyed one another's company. On the way home, he asked if I was ready to try skydiving next. I told him I had always wanted to try it but was too scared. I explained that the only way I would try skydiving was if I lost all will to live. He smiled. He didn't flinch. He didn't look guilty or uncomfortable. Nothing indicated to me that he had lost all will to live. He was dead five days later.

The last email I ever wrote to my husband was sent three days prior to his death. It read as follows:

It's been a while since I wrote you an email. Since you are picking up the kids I thought this was a good time! I just wanted to let you know how much I am enjoying our adventures. I really love that you are excited and interested in things that I find exciting and interesting (yoga and walking for example!). I also really enjoyed our naughty nap this morning. Lying next to you has taken on a new meaning and pleasure. I hope your session with your new therapist was helpful today. I hope you are able to learn things about yourself and find a happiness within that I was not able to give to you. I also hope that you have realized how I have

come out of my comfort zone to be with you. I never would have gotten on a four-seater airplane in the past!
I am looking forward to more adventures! I love you. -D

The last email my husband ever wrote me was sent on a Thursday, he was dead that Saturday afternoon.

I am so glad we're together and we share the dream. I am so grateful you're giving me the chance to recapture missed opportunities to show you that I think you're beautiful inside and out, and that you're very special to me.
I love you.

Friday was a bad day for me. I had my first therapy session with my new psychologist. My husband had sought him out because our marriage counselor was good at helping us work on our marriage problems, but we were dealing with depression and internal issues that we both acknowledged we needed to address privately with a Ph.D. psychologist. I was extremely depressed. I had terrible mood swings. He would call it whiplash, because I would be high as a kite and enjoying each other and then on a dime I would sink into a deep depression. I would verbally attack him, call him just about every name in the book, and would give up hope on our marriage. I had suspected that he was having an affair that year but he always denied it. I thought if I let him know that I knew, he would cut the shit and we would never have to address it. But he couldn't stop. Even when he knew I knew. He was so cruel and mean, talking and texting her during our dates and family outings. He thought I was stupid. I remember going to church begging God for the sign. I had to know if I was losing my mind or if my husband was cheating. As fate would have it, I caught him red-handed. We had purchased new iPhones and his text messages were being mistakenly routed to my twelve-year old daughter's phone. She thought the texts were between him and I. Boy was she wrong. We never figured out how the text messages got crossed but I know it was the sign I had begged God to send me.

It was four and a half months ago; he was away on business the evening I found out. When the affair was finally confirmed, my words to him where, "You are a liar, a drunk and a cheat. Don't come home."

She could have him. I was not putting up a fight. Well the moment the cat was out of the bag, the affair ended. He dumped his whore like a hot potato and ran home to me and the kids. I took him back for the sake of the kids. But I was not making it easy on him. I was so angry, so depressed and miserable. My world had been torn apart. I had met my therapist for the first time that Friday. My husband's last session with him was two days prior on Wednesday. His parting words to our therapist that day, "So Dr. M, do you think you can help my wife?"

We later speculated that he had no intention of getting help for himself; he just wanted to get me connected with a competent psychologist. He never told the doctor he was having suicidal thoughts. He never asked for help.

During my first individual therapy session on Friday afternoon, my shrink explained that it was ok to be angry. I took him up on it and I was angry from the

moment I left the session and my husband never saw me smile again.
 I was lying in bed Friday night and I was violently angry, my husband walked into the room to say good night. I looked at him and said, "Maybe since your whore is the size of a man I am really not what you need." I am petite (downright short to be honest) and my size has always been an issue for me. It just hurt so bad that my husband decided to cheat on me with a woman who is 5'10. A height I would have killed for! And as a middle-aged woman, I was really hurt that his whore was twelve years younger than him. Women always know when their significant other has been cheating. Men don't realize it but they are different. Men are different in their behavior, different in their personality, different in bed. And I saw that difference in my own husband of sixteen years at the time. "I am not a fucking fagot!" he cried as his face turned red and he banged his head as hard as he could against his cherry wood armoire like a child then he stormed out of the room.
 I was a little taken aback because I had never heard him use that unacceptable word or act so violent, I knew I pushed a button. I shut my eyes and went to sleep.
 I woke up Saturday morning. He wasn't in bed next to me. I got a strange feeling in my gut. I got out of bed, walked into the kitchen and was relieved when I noticed him lying on the couch reading a book. I coldly said good morning and kept walking. I got myself a cup of coffee and went back to bed. I was depressed.
 He finished his book, went out and bought the kids bagels for breakfast and Starbucks coffee for him and me. When he came home he watched a movie with the kids and I remained in bed for hours. I finally pulled myself

out of bed. I heated up the cold Starbucks and sat outside. It was an overcast, rainy day. He followed me out. We talked. I was such a bitch. We had been married for seventeen and a half years. He asked if I would renew our wedding vows at our twentieth wedding anniversary. I said, "Renew our wedding vows? Are you crazy? I wouldn't have married you in the first place."

After some negotiation, I said that I would renew our vows at twenty-five years if our marriage lasted. As far as I was concerned, our marriage was not going to last. I did promise him that I would give the marriage one year before filing for divorce to see if we could work it out. Although I intended on keeping my promise, he only gave me four and a half months to work it out. We talked about other things as well. His job wasn't going very well. He was given a promotion but, as a result of the promotion, he had lost his team and was back in an individual contributor role. He had a huge ego and enjoyed being in charge of a team. Although the promotion was a nice raise and a higher title, he knew in his heart that he was being put out to "corporate pasture". He admitted that people were beginning to talk about his inappropriate relationship with his whore who was also his co-worker. As they did little to hide it, they even shared hotel rooms during large work conventions. I am sure many people knew exactly what was going on. He drank a lot. He was always the life of the party but in the corporate world, you really do not want the reputation of being the office drunk. During our last conversation, I reminded him that he did not deserve his promotion. He knew I was right. Not only had he given up his whore the day he got caught, he also never took another sip of alcohol.

I interrogated him about his affair. I demanded answers to questions like, "How many times did you tell her you loved her? Why don't you just get back on the plane and go back to her? Your daughters and I deserve better".

He was sorry. He really was sincerely sorry. He just wanted to hear me say, *I forgive you*. But I couldn't do it.

During that last conversation, he admitted that he started seeing the new psychologist (the doctor I had seen the previous day), because he was having dark thoughts and thinking of suicide. He had mentioned the term *dark thoughts* to me during prior arguments but I didn't take him seriously. I thought he was acting like a child and trying to manipulate me by diverting my anger away from his affair. He never mentioned the word *suicide* to me before. I later spoke to the psychologist and he confirmed that although my husband may have told me that he came to see him for suicidal thoughts, he never mentioned it to him. He would have been put on a suicide plan but he never sought out the help.

We sat outside and drank our coffee, I was being impossible and he rightfully got angry with me. He got up, whispered something inaudible to me, and said he loved me, kissed me on my lips, and stormed into the house. I never saw him alive again.

I sat outside and stared at the rain and spoke to my children as they came in and out of the patio door. At least forty-five minutes later, assuming he was working in his office upstairs or watching television with the kids in the family room, I crawled into our bedroom and got back into bed. I noticed that the bedroom door was closed. It wasn't locked and I walked in to lie down. I was not really sleeping but not really awake. I was so depressed that I felt like an elephant was sitting on me. I couldn't move. I just rested.

Chapter Two: The Closet

    I heard a strange noise that I thought was coming from my window. I just assumed it was an animal outside. I didn't think too much about it. I wish I had. After at least forty-five minutes of lying down I decided I had to get up, take a shower and talk to him. I had to talk to him about his admission of thoughts of suicide and try to continue with the healing process. It was now about one o'clock in the afternoon. I was still in my nightclothes, a black nightshirt and no bra. I grabbed a pair of clean shorts, t-shirt, underwear and bra. There was a little hallway leading from our master bedroom where I had been lying in bed, leading to our large master bathroom. The "his" and "hers" closets were located on the left side of the small hallway. I walked past them as I headed toward the bathroom to finally take my shower. As a walked toward the shower I thought that it was strange that my husband's florescent closet light was on and his closet door was partially closed. His closet door was always open and his light was never on. As I approached I got another really weird feeling in my gut. As a passed the closet, I glanced into the closet. I saw a pair of blue feet. I gasped, dropped my clothes all over the floor and then I saw the image that will haunt me until the day I die. My husband of seventeen years was hanging by the neck, knees off of the floor from a brown leather belt fastened to the top wire shelf of his closet. My husband hanged himself and I was lying on the bed only about eight feet away.
    He looked so small. The look on his face was peaceful. Whatever pain he was in was definitely gone. His pain left his body and was immediately transferred to

my family and me. There was no evidence on his face that he had been crying or upset. There didn't even seem to be any sweat beads on his forehead. He chose the method of a soft hang or partial hang. He was not fully suspended off the ground, but was hanging by the neck in a kneeling position. I often wonder what was going through his head as he lost consciousness. He could have easily changed his mind and simply put his feet down and stood up to relieve the stress on his neck. Clearly he was determined. He was fully dressed, wearing a pair of black shorts and a red t-shirt, his Celtic cross necklace and no wedding ring. I grabbed him and tried to loosen the belt around his neck by unfastening the buckle. But he had the belt rigged in such a way that the buckle was the noose, and the strap was fastened to the wire shelf by what must have been a screw. I tried to pick him up but he was too heavy. I couldn't unfasten him off of the noose.

    I didn't scream. My first thought was that I had to protect my kids. My daughters were watching television in the family room. I ran toward my bedroom door, slammed and locked it and grabbed my cell phone, which was luckily in the bedroom on my dresser. I dialed what I thought was 911. I told the woman I thought my husband was dead and he had hanged himself in the closet. The woman cut me off and said something like "Lord Jesus, this is 411, God help you child." I said "Oh shit" as I hung up the phone and then dialed 911. I reiterated my situation. They were sending help. The 911 operator offered to walk me through CPR. I explained that I knew CPR but he was still hanging. She yelled, "Cut him down NOW."

I said "How? He is so heavy and the belt won't come off."

"Get a knife, quickly," she ordered. I ran out of the room, slammed the door behind me and sprinted to the kitchen. I grabbed two knives out of the knife block. One of the knives was a gift from his best friend.

I hear, "Mommy what are you doing?"

"Nothing", I said as I sprinted out of the kitchen with the knives.

I am short, not even 5 feet, 110 pounds. The belt was fastened at least six feet high. As I ran out of the kitchen with the knives, I passed the den on the way to my bedroom. Luckily there just happened to be a kitchen chair in the den because the kids needed an extra chair in the office to work on the computer. I grabbed the chair and brought it with me into the closet. I climbed up on the chair and cut the noose with one strong swoop. My 190-pound husband came crashing down on me. He landed and hurt my leg but I was able to get him on the floor while protecting his head and I began CPR. 911 was still on speakerphone. I started CPR. That is when I remembered that I had an AED. It was located past my front door in a linen closet. Again I ran out of the room, grabbed the AED and unlocked and slightly opened the front door. I didn't want the police to ring the doorbell. I slammed and locked the bedroom door and tried the AED. It didn't work. I still don't know if it didn't work because the batteries were old, but I suspect that my husband was already dead and there was no heart activity for the AED to zap. I later told my children that I grabbed the knives because I needed them to cut off his shirt in order to perform CPR and hook up the AED. That was the first of many lies yet to come.

Because we have a swimming pool, the alarm beeps when the doors are opened. I heard the front door beep and I ran to meet the police officer. I quickly led him to the bedroom. He continued the CPR process. I kept asking him, "Is he dead?"

He assured me that they can do a lot to bring him back. "How long as he been like this?"

I had no idea. I kept saying "Forty-five minutes."

But I really don't know when he hanged himself. Was it while I was still outside drinking coffee in the rain or while I was a few feet away listening to television? I was calm. I was completely numb. I was in shock. I felt like I was in an episode of a drama television show that I often watch. It wasn't real. Eventually the cavalry came. It was horrible. As the cops pulled me out of the closet I remember yelling at him, "If you're not dead I am going to kill you."

It seemed like an eternity but additional police officers and EMT workers eventually showed up. They rushed me off to the living room to sit with the kids and keep them secure in the living room. I don't know if it was divine intervention or pure fright, but my children just sat on the couch and watched TV. They didn't ask questions, they didn't scream, they just sat there and no one spoke.

At one point, I got off of the couch and went into my bedroom to check on the EMTs. My husband was just lying on the floor. I screamed, "Can't you zap him and wake him up?"

The EMT yelled back, "There is nothing to zap." Again they asked, "How long has he been like this?"

I answered, "I don't know! I thought he was upstairs doing work in his office!"

Again I asked if he was dead. They wouldn't answer me and explained that he needed to be taken to the hospital. The police officer asked if I had any family or friends to help me with the children while I went to the hospital. I explained that I had no one. My parents and sister were several hours away and I had no friends as we had lived in our neighborhood only a short amount of time. I said that I would just leave my twelve-year-old in charge. I was in shock. I didn't think my husband and I would be stuck at the hospital for too long once they got him going again. The police officer explained that I could not leave the children alone and they could not be in the house.

I ran outside to look for someone, anyone. In a normally active neighborhood, not one person was out. Everyone locked themselves in their homes. I was alone. There were cop cars, ambulances, and emergency vehicles surrounding my home, and not one person to help me. I received a text. It was my neighbor up the street. She was the only decent person in the entire neighborhood. It read, *Are you ok?*

I replied, *No. I need help.* She ran down the street to help. It was decided that she would take my children to her house. My kids were no longer allowed in the house because they were not allowed to be there during the investigation. Investigation? What?

By the Grace of God, my children never saw the horror of their father's dead body. I shudder to think of what could have happened if one of my kids found him instead of me. There were no restrictions in our house that would have prevented one of the kids from meandering into my bathroom, passing by the closet where he hanged. I am convinced that if they had found him, I would be writing this book by their bedside located in a mental institution.

As my daughters, ages twelve, ten and eight left to go to the neighbor's house they asked me if everything was going to be ok. I responded, "Daddy is very sick, say your prayers."

I stood in my home, loaded with emergency personnel, wearing nothing but a nightshirt and underwear. I hadn't even brushed my teeth yet. It was after three in the afternoon. I realized that I couldn't go to the hospital dressed the way I was. I grabbed a pair of shorts, shirt and a bra and headed to my bathroom. That's where I was stopped. I was not allowed in my bathroom until the investigation was completed. I complied and simply stripped and dressed in front of the cop. I just didn't even care at that point. Before I was cleared to leave for the hospital I had to turn over his phone, my phone and his driver's license and answer some questions. The first question was the most obvious and yet impossible to answer. "What happened?"

I answered honestly, "I have no fucking idea, I was in a bad mood." I explained we were having marital problems.

"Didn't you see the belt in his closet?" the cop asked.

I responded, "I don't know. It's a closet. He has a ton of belts in there." I had no recollection if I had seen the belt or not hanging from the top shelf. If I had, it wouldn't have struck me as odd. It was his favorite belt and all of his other belts were hanging from the lower wire rack. The police officer later told my sister that the investigators determined that the belt had been rigged in the closet for a while.

The police returned my phone to me so I could call my family. I called my mom and dad. My mother answered the phone. "Hi! Is everything ok?" she asked.

I replied "No. I need you to come down right away. The kids are ok, it is my husband."

She replied "What? What is all that noise?"

"The cops," I answered. She later admitted that the first thought that went through her head was that I did something to hurt my husband. Never would she have thought he would hurt himself. "He tried to kill himself."

I heard a scream and my father came on the line. "What is going on?"

I explained to my father that my husband tried to kill himself in the closet. He was being taken to the hospital. My parents arrived at my home at two am that night and my sister a little earlier at eleven pm.

I was not crying, I was not screaming, I simply remember looking at one of the EMT workers who was bent over my husband on the floor. I looked at him and said "Oh fuck."

He looked up at me and responded, "Yeah, oh fuck is right."

The police would not permit me to travel in the ambulance with my husband. In hindsight, I believe that the police and medical personnel were protecting my children and I by not pronouncing my husband dead at the house. The neighbor's husband, whom I didn't know very well at the time, drove me to the hospital. When I arrived at the hospital, the hospital staff made me wait in the waiting room for what seemed like hours. I was not allowed to see my husband until it was cleared by the police. I sat in the waiting room and just prayed. I prayed to God that he would be ok, but I knew what I saw and I knew he was dead. My stomach started to rumble and I found myself running to the bathroom. I wasn't able to keep food in my stomach for the next several weeks.

Finally, a police officer came into the waiting room to get me and escort me into the emergency room. I was brought, not to my husband's bedside, but instead into a doctor's lounge. A doctor and a nurse sat me down and told me that my husband was dead.

"Are you sure?" I calmly asked. "There must be a mistake, can you try a little harder to wake him up?"

"I am so sorry, but no. He is gone." Said the doctor.

"What am I supposed to tell my children?"

The nurse replied, "You have to tell them that he was very sick."

And then the questions started again, "What happened?" Again I explained that I was in a bad mood. We were having serious marital problems.

I was still calm. I was not crying. I was in shock and denial.

In walked the detective. The room cleared and he sat down with his pad. "What happened?"

For the third time, I had to explain to a complete stranger that I didn't know what happened, I was in a bad mood because I had caught my husband cheating on me. We were having marital problems. He wanted to hear me say that I forgave him but I wasn't ready.

Then he asked, "Why were there knives in the closet?"

I numbly explained the knives were there because the 911 woman told me to cut him down with a knife, so I grabbed two because I didn't know which one was sharp enough to cut through the leather belt.

He continued to interrogate me, "Why was there a chair in the closet?" Did he put it in there?"

"No." I explained, "I grabbed the chair because he was too high for me to cut him down, I couldn't reach without it." Thinking back, I think I was under suspicion because it was clear by my husband's blue legs that he had not hanged from kicking away a chair. I guess they had to make sure I didn't stage the suicide. I shudder to think what would have happened to my kids if I were falsely accused of hurting him. I guess my husband of seventeen years never thought of that either.

The detective put his pen down, looked at me and said, "Would you like to see your husband now?"

"Yes." I said.

Still calm and stone faced, I followed him through the hallway; all eyes were on me as we passed the nurses' station. The detective and I entered my husband's room. He looked like he was sleeping. He still had the breathing tube in his mouth, so it made him appear as if he was smiling. He looked peaceful. I looked at him and said, "I'm sorry. I forgive you." I started shaking him and yelling, "You can wake up now." I shook him harder, "Wake up, I forgive you. Wake up, I'm sorry." I was screaming and crying at the same time, "Wake up, please. I'M SORRY. PLEASE, I FORGIVE YOU, GET UP SO WE CAN GO HOME."

I remember hearing a little voice next to me saying to the detective "Why is she saying she is sorry?"

The detective placed his hand on my arm. "Come on, dear, we have to go."

I looked at him and said, "No, that's ok, I'll wait here with my husband." I didn't want to leave him there alone. For the last seventeen years I was always by his side.

He replied, "We have to go now dear, he is going to get cold."

He escorted me out of the emergency room, past the nurse's station again, I was absolutely hysterical crying and screaming. I would never see my husband again.

As we got into the parking lot, the detective told me that I needed to go back to my neighbor's home. My neighbor waited at the hospital with me while his wife watched my children. I explained to the detective that I really didn't know my neighbor very well. "Could you just give me a ride home?" I politely asked the police detective.

"No", he explained. "Your house is a crime scene and I have to go there to complete my investigation."

I walked into the parking lot, called my mother and told her my husband was gone. During that conversation, my mother planted the seed. "You can't tell the kids what happened. You can't tell anyone the truth".

It was around 5:00 pm after I left the hospital. With nowhere to go, I asked my neighbor if he could drive me to church. I am a member of a not-so-friendly Catholic Church. I knew it was around time for Saturday evening Mass and I was hoping to speak with a priest. I arrived at the tail end of Mass. It was just about time for communion. I took communion and waited for Mass to end. I needed to speak to a priest. I waited patiently for Father G to greet all of the parishioners after mass. I politely asked him if I could speak with him for a moment.

"I am busy, can't it wait?"

This priest was a visiting priest and not a full-time member of the church. "No," I said. "It is urgent".

Annoyed, we sat down together in a pew. I explained that my husband had just passed away. I didn't know what to do. He asked me how.

I answered truthfully, "Suicide."

Then he looked at me. "Don't I know you? I have already talked to you at another church."

"No" I answered. "We have never spoken before."

"Well" he answered, "Suicide? I don't go for that." He continued, "What do you expect me to do about it? I can't give him last rites because he is already dead. Call the office on Monday and you can make funeral arrangements with the office."

To give him the benefit of the doubt, I thought maybe he didn't believe me. I was in shock, I wasn't crying and my demeanor was calm. Maybe he mistook me for some nut job he had spoken to at another church. I have no idea. I looked at him and said, "What I am supposed to tell my children?"

He said, "I don't know. I can't help you. What I am supposed to do?"

I looked at him and said "Nothing. Please just pray for me and my three children." I calmly got up and walked out. He just watched me walk away.

When I returned to the car, my neighbor who was patiently waiting for me in the car, said, "How did it go?" I said I spoke to a priest.

He said, "Oh, that's good."

I said, "Not really, he was kind of an asshole."

"Oh?" He said with a puzzled look on his face. As we drove back to my home, I begin to think, if a priest could have that kind of unsympathetic heartless reaction to my husband's suicide, what the hell would everyone else do? That's when I decided my mother was right, I couldn't tell anyone. I couldn't put my kids through the humiliation of what I had just been through with that horrible priest.

Ironically, about six months later, a friend of mine from my kids' school had a Mass said for my husband at a neighboring Catholic Church. I had never attended that church before, but son of a bitch, if it wasn't Father G who said my husband's mass. I stared him down the entire service. During Mass, not only did I pray for myself, my kids, my dead husband, but I also prayed for that priest. Clearly, he needed prayers too. After Mass, he just smiled at me. Not a devious smile. He smiled a sincere smile. I forgave that priest for being so terrible to me. I actually think it was God's way of giving me a green light to invent the lie. If Father G had been kind to me, the decision to create the lie would have been much more difficult.

My neighbor dropped me home, the crime scene tape had been removed and I was cleared to re-enter my house. It was around seven pm. I was back in an empty house. The knives were put back into the knife block and the chair was put away by the police and the only evidence of the horror that had taken place was the AED and my clothes thrown all over the floor of my husband's closet. My husband was dead, my kids were at the neighbor's house, and my family was en route. The only person to keep me company was the police officer. For my safety, the police would not leave me unsupervised until my family arrived. I remember watching the police officer as he gazed at my beautiful family portrait. I had a beautiful family. I was once blessed with three wonderful children and an adoring husband. I often wonder what he must have been thinking as he started at the photo. When my sister finally arrived that night, the police officer explained to her that it was one of the worst scenes he had experienced. Hardly ever do men commit suicide with their wife and children in the home.

After my neighbor dropped me off, he went home and watched my children at his house while his wife switched and also came over to my home to comfort me and relieve the police until my family arrived. Thankfully she brought tissues with her because I had none. We got to converse and she, too, asked me, "What happened?"

Again I explained that I was in a bad mood. We were having marital problems. By this time, I think I had told about eight strangers all of my private marital problems. I was going back and forth from completely calm to hysterics. At one point, I recall looking at her and saying "I don't think he is really dead. Can you just do me a favor and go look in the bedroom, I think he is in there."

She looked at me and said, "He is not in there."

"Please," I begged, "Just go double check. I think he is in there."

She got up and walked into my bedroom and rechecked the closet. "No," she said, "He's not here."

"Ok, thanks for looking," I said. "Let me check just in case." I got up and walked into my marital bedroom. It was empty.

No tragedy would be complete without a nosey neighbor in the mix…and in she walks. "Is everything ok?" asks the nosey neighbor as my "good" neighbor and I sit on the couch in my living room.

I explained that my husband had a heart attack. Lie number one was complete. She stayed a little while and pried into my personal business. I never had another conversation with her. She never checked up on me, my children or offered any kind of help or assistance. She only lived a couple of houses away and it would not have been an effort to see how I was doing. I guess she was just fishing for information so she could tell the entire neighborhood. And she did. I later found out that word did get out into my neighborhood that there was a suicide. I didn't know too many people but I can say that although people may have enjoyed having something to talk about, with the exception of my neighbors who watched my children and took me to the hospital, not one person offered condolences or offered to help me in any way. I wonder if they would have shown any compassion if there were not suicide rumors. I quickly put the house on the market and got the hell out of that neighborhood.

It was about 9:30 pm when my phone rang. I answered the phone and was told that my husband was an organ donor. Did I want to fulfill his wishes? I thought about it for a moment and said, "Yes. I do."

The man on the phone explained that he had several questions he needed to ask me as part of the organ donating process. Little did I know I would be on the phone for over an hour answering more personal questions. As he began to explain the process, I cut him off, "Wait." I said. "I think there might be a mistake. I don't think he is really dead. Can you just double check and call me back?"

"No ma'am," he said. "I am awfully sorry, but there is no mistake."

He continued to ask me about my husband's travel history. That is when I realized that my husband had traveled the world without me, he traveled the world with another woman. He then asked me about his sexual history. This is when I began to realize that I had absolutely no idea who he was. Who was this person who was capable of hanging himself in our home with the children in another room?

My answers changed from definitive yes's and no's to "not to my knowledge."

I hoped that by following through with my husband's wishes to be an organ donor, that someone, if not multiple people benefited from our loss.... Maybe God let him die because he needed the organs for someone else. I don't know, but God has a plan. Maybe one day I will figure out his plan.

I do know there is someone out there walking around with my husband's eye tissue. The only organization I received a thank you note from was from the eye donor organization. I thought it was a little strange but nice when they sent me a thank you letter and a key chain. Although I had no intention of using the key chain, I did save it with the thought of maybe giving it to my kids one day once they understood the great gift of organ donation. Several months after my husband passed away, I received another letter from this organization. This letter I found to be completely bizarre. It was an invitation to a picnic. Every year the organization throws a picnic for the families of the donators and the recipients of eye tissue donors. I was alone at the time I read it once and then again. "What the fuck?" I said out loud to myself as I sat alone in an empty house. "I can't believe I just got invited to a thank you for giving us your dead husband's eyeball party." I threw the invitation out and had another sleepless night.

It must have been around 10:30 pm when I finally got off the phone with the organ donor organization. I received a text from my middle daughter who was still stuck at the neighbor's house with my other two daughters. *Is daddy ok?* It read. I ignored the text and did not answer back. I was not going to ruin my children's last night of childhood. I wasn't going to lie and say everything was ok and I sure as hell wasn't going to tell them the truth.

At around eleven pm my sister arrived and relieved my neighbor and the cops for the evening. My parents later arrived at two am. I just cried all night. I cried myself to sleep on the couch for an hour or two.

Chapter Three: The Lie

This email was written about a month prior to my husband's suicide.

>   *Hi! I went through my morning routine of beating myself up and I was feeling antsy so I came down and pressed the coffee button. Now I'm down here counting the minutes until our morning coffee and I'm missing you terribly.*
>   *To keep myself occupied I've been reading Gottman blogs and sincerely racking my brain for things I can be doing better and more of. It was so good to have belly laughs with you yesterday; not just to watch them, but to be part of them with you and your parents.*
>   *I love you, totally, completely, with every fiber of my being. I love being in a place where we are addressing problems in a way we never did. I love our new habits. I am committed to rebuilding our relationship and making it better than ever. I know you're here with me and you're working hard, too. I know we're connected and working together again. I love that you have hope...this fills me with energy and enthusiasm.*
>   *I look forward to our journey together. We have many good years ahead at our disposal.*
>   *Thank you for being so strong and*

supportive, and for being such a great mother.
I love you. I look forward to showing you for another 30+ years.

In accordance with our marriage therapy, we were building good habits and enjoying our time together. We really enjoyed our morning coffee time. He would make the coffee and we would spend some time together sitting outside, talking, before the kids woke up. It was fun and we were enjoying our coffee time.

I woke up on the couch the morning after his death. I started screaming, "It's time for coffee! Where are you?" I searched the house for him. I searched his office, our bedroom, his closet and every bathroom. My father found me when I was in the garage searching the cars for him. I was screaming at the top of my lungs. "ITS TIME FOR COFFEE GOD DAMNIT."

I looked at my father and there were tears in his eyes. "Please," he cried. "If anything happens to you I wouldn't be able to survive. I will die too."

I think he thought I too was losing my mind.

I had to get control of myself because my kids were coming home soon. But where was the note? There must be a note. My sister asked the police officer and they confirmed that no note was found during their investigation. Before my kids came home, I had to find that note. It must be here. He had to have told me why. Me, my father, mother and sister searched the entire house. We looked in every pocket of every piece of clothing in his closet, we searched every drawer in the entire house, we searched his car, we searched the garage, we pulled his desk apart, I thumbed through every book he owned, I looked under the bed, in the medicine cabinet even the kitchen. I checked his phone. There was no note on the phone. He made no calls that day. He did not call anyone to say goodbye. He did not call anyone to ask for help. Looking back for some strange reason, I think he thought I knew why. I never stopped looking for that note. The search continued for the next eleven months. I did find his wedding ring. He left it neatly placed on the kitchen counter next to his car keys.

Before I told my daughters that their father was dead, I went into my room, grabbed my statue of the Blessed Mother, hugged and kissed her and prayed for strength and guidance as I was about to have the most difficult conversation with my daughters that I probably would ever have in my entire life. My three daughters ages twelve, ten and eight arrived home at about 10:00am. They were happy to see my parents and my sister. "Where's Daddy, is he ok?" they asked.

The seven of us sat on the couches in the family room. This was a beautiful room with brown leather couches in front of large beautiful windows. I told my daughters that daddy was very sick and we didn't know it. He died and he is with God in heaven. He is no longer sick and he was never in pain. He will always love us and will always look after us. You can still talk to him in your prayers.

The kids were crying and screaming and it was totally and completely heartbreaking. How could he do this to them I thought. "But Daddy was fine yesterday," said my middle child. "He watched a movie with us."

Then I hear my youngest daughter, "Look" she said with an excited voice between sniffles. "A rainbow."

We all looked outside and the most beautiful rainbow shined through the floor-to-ceiling windows. The irony was that there was no rain, just a rainbow. We all agreed that it was daddy and he was fine and that was his way of telling us. On the one-year anniversary of his death he sent us another rainbow.

It was time to start making phone calls. I had to protect my children. My parents, sister and I hatched the lie. Go with heart attack and don't give out too much information. Don't answer specific questions. If people start asking detailed questions, and they will, tell them that we don't want to talk about it. When you hatch a lie, it is very important not to give up too many details. The less you say, the less likely you are to get caught in the lie. We thought for sure people would be suspicious. Young men just don't drop dead. But no one questioned it. It was the easiest lie we ever had to tell. No one would have believed the truth. My husband was the life of the party. He was always happy, funny and easy going. He rarely lost his temper. He was extremely smart and successful. He had it all. He and I never fought. He had a great relationship with my parents and my family. Things were a little rocky recently with him and my family because of his affair. My sister was recently divorced due to infidelity on her husband's side and it tore our family apart. My husband was always put up on a pedestal. He would never do anything to hurt his family. He was a great father and a great husband…until he wasn't. My family was very disappointed with him because of his affair, but for the sake of the children they had to forgive him. Everyone was trying to keep our family together. It was time to tell everyone my husband was dead. My father made the calls. The lie was in play and there was no going back. We all agreed that keeping the cause of my husband's death a secret was absolutely the best possible thing for my children. Dead is dead. Will my husband be less dead if I tell people the truth? No. Is it really anyone's business how or why a person dies? When a young man dies out of the blue it is only normal for people to wonder why. I get that. People ask, not because they can somehow help (because let's face it, by then it is too late). They ask because they are concerned with their own mortality, or it's just morbid curiosity. They think, *if this young man can drop dead, can I?* It is a scary thought. At first, I felt really uncomfortable about lying. Since then, I have become quite an expert at it. Think about it, at the end of the day, does it really matter to anyone else why my husband is dead? No matter if I lie or tell the truth, dead is still dead and no truth will bring him back.

Lying is my gift. It is the last gift I will ever give my husband. It is a gift to my children, my husband's sister, his best friend and his co-workers and friends, even his whore. I checked his phone, his computer emails, and texts and there was no indication that he tried to say goodbye or ask anyone for help. There were no phone calls made from his phone that day or in the minutes prior to his death. How do you think his sister and his best friend would feel knowing that he didn't think to ask them for help? Their guilt would be unbearable. I know because my guilt certainly is.

He was a great guy. I don't know if he wanted people to know he committed suicide or if he would have appreciated this cover-up. I choose to protect his legacy.

I don't want people to remember him as the son-of-a-bitch who hanged himself in the closet for no reason with his kids in the house. When people think of him or remember him, they think of the good times. I want them to remember the fun, the laughs, the love, and the work. That would all be forgotten with the knowledge of the suicide. He deserves better than that. I don't know what really happened to him. But I know he was sick. He needed help and failed to get it. My children deserve better. They do not need to grow up being *the kids whose dad killed himself.* That is a stigma that's extremely difficult to shake off. My children need to grow up knowing their dad loved them. They are much too young to understand mental illness, affairs, and possible child abuse. I can't risk the possibility of my kids thinking that their father didn't love them. I often lie awake asking myself *am I that bad that my husband would rather be dead than be with me?* My job is to keep a very close eye on my kids' mental health. I realize the importance of that. Me not telling them is not a "sweeping under the rug" or not wanting to have to "deal with it". It is for their protection. PERIOD. I refuse to apologize. I am very comfortable with my choice of keeping it a secret.

About nine months prior, we found out that our fifteen-year-old dog had cancer. On the day of the diagnosis I got a very bad feeling. I felt as if this was the beginning of the end of a very long good ride. Things were going good, too good. I was happy. We had recently moved into a beautiful home, my kids loved their school, I was no longer working, my husband was having an affair but I didn't know it yet. My fake life was perfect. I was terrified that something was going to happen to one of my aging parents. But I never saw this coming. My husband was drinking and sleeping with another woman, but I was too focused on the dog. Let's face it; I had her almost as long as I had my husband. Maybe I shouldn't have slept so often on the couch with her when he was home. He would usually stay on the couch with me, but it still wasn't the same as sharing a marital bed. The dog's treatment was on me. I had to drive an hour to take her to chemotherapy. I remember calling him from the highway, hysterical. The doctor told me that there was nothing that could be done for the dog. She was dying.

He was away on business. I could barely breathe, I was crying so hard on the phone while driving. Did he come home to be with me? No, of course not. I would never even suggest or expect him to. Did he spend the night with his whore living it up? Yep! Another morning the dog had a seizure prior to him leaving on a business trip. I found out later that the trip was optional and he probably could have stayed home with me. But he didn't. He left me home alone with our dying dog and spent the next three nights with his whore. I guess it is just the lack of empathy that pisses me off so much. Anyway, after he was "caught", he spent a lot more time at home. One night, in the middle of a family dinner, my husband, our three daughters and I were enjoying my home cooked dinner. I gave the dog some table scraps. She gobbled it up, keeled over and died in front of the entire family. My husband got his white dress shirt, gently laid it over the dog and we said a prayer as a family. I told him that I was glad he was there when the dog passed and I wasn't alone. After my husband died I buried my dog's ashes with his ashes. After the fact, he felt very guilty and ashamed that he wasn't there for the dog and I. It was my way of making it up to him. At least I know they are not alone. I lost two best friends in a couple of months. Death entered our home and didn't leave. My daughters experienced horror of seeing their beloved dog dead on the floor. I wasn't going to let that happen again. I had my husband's body cremated.

I was feeling so guilty. I know I was in such a bad mood the day he died. I felt I bullied my husband into killing himself. I needed forgiveness. I was so sorry. My husband was dead, my children didn't have a father, and it was all my fault. I needed to speak to a compassionate priest. I called my favorite priest, the only priest I ever had a friendship with. He dropped everything to see me.

I spilled my guts. "I read texts between him and his girlfriend and he was like a stranger. They read like two middle-school children flirting with each other. They called each other Sweet Bear. He never called me pet names. It was weird. I didn't even know him. He was a stranger to me. Father, I was so angry at him that I think at some point I wished he was dead," I admitted. "I never told him I wished he was dead or told him to kill himself. But what if he could read my mind? What if God heard my thoughts and took my husband from me? There were signs and I ignored them. He told me he was having dark thoughts and I didn't take him seriously. He told me he felt like he had PTSD. I said and did nothing. I actually got angry but I didn't want to start another fight. I was angry that he would compare himself getting caught screwing a co-worker to a brave soldier. I called him every name in the book. I even called him the "P" word. I didn't think he was much of a man and I told him so. When I knew I had pressed a button that made him upset, rather than backing down, I pushed harder. I kept pushing. I felt like there was something more I needed to know. If I pushed hard enough, we could talk about it. I pushed too hard. I think I bullied my husband into killing himself. There were a couple of occasions that I got really weird uncomfortable feelings in my gut. Maybe God was trying to talk to me. I should have acted on them. I should have talked to him about it. I was so mad and too selfish to put my feelings aside. I need God to forgive me. I am so sorry." I continued as I cried, "I know my husband was sorry for the affair. He went to confession and apologized to me. He just wanted to hear that I forgave him. I couldn't do it. I wasn't ready. I had an inappropriate relationship behind my husband's back fourteen years ago, before we had children. I was so ashamed and sorry. I went to confession and begged God for forgiveness. I never told my husband until the day I caught him having the affair. I thought if I told him, we could get the guilt off of our chests and try to repair our marriage. If I hadn't done that several years ago, I don't think I would have been able to find it in my heart to try to forgive him. I think telling him made it worse. Yes, I told him because I wanted to hurt him, but I also wanted to repair our marriage. I loved him and I love my family." By now I was hysterical, "I AM TERRIFIED THAT HE IS BURNING IN HELL. HE DOESN'T DESERVE IT. I AM SO SORRY, THIS IS ALL MY FAULT. GOD FORGIVE ME."

    Father listened to all I had to say and then said, "Men make bad choices. It is not unusual for a man to start an affair and act like a teenager." He continued, "What your husband did was his choice. He was sick. God forgives him. You have absolutely NOTHING to feel guilty about."

I also told him that I had made a decision to lie to everyone. Including my children. I said I wasn't sorry for the lie and I am not asking for forgiveness. He understood my position, and said that there may be a day when I may have to tell my kids. I pray there never is. He said I didn't need it, but he took my confession and gave me absolution anyway.

His parting message to me was, "Promise me you will let go of the guilt. Your husband made his own choices and he is with God. God forgives him. He is at peace."

Till this day I wish I could let go of the guilt and keep my promise to Father.

Word spread like wild fire and friends and colleagues of my husband were making arrangements from all over the world to pay their respects and Facebook was going crazy. While my family made all of the funeral arrangements, I sat on the couch in an almost catatonic state and cried all day and night. My one and only task was to deal with his company's human resource department. There were many people from my husband's company asking where to send flowers or money to my children. I didn't want flowers. I didn't even want a damn funeral but I had to keep up appearances and give my children closure. Under the Human Resource's advice, a "Go Fund Me Account" was set up. People from all over the world sent money to my children. The notes of love and gratitude and sympathy were overwhelming. My husband helped launch a lot of people's careers and helped many more move forward and people were grateful for knowing him and having him in their lives. I was humiliated. I had never asked anyone for money ever in my entire life. People who I knew had much less than me sent money. My guilt grew. Would they still send the money if they knew it was a suicide? I was sitting alone reading my emails when I was alerted that a GO FUND ME contribution came in. I looked to see who was the generous person who sent my kids $500. It was my husband's whore. Suddenly my sorrow and grief turned to rage. Alone in the house I screamed at the top of my lungs. "I FUCKING HATE YOU. HOW CAN YOU DO THIS TO ME?" I cried and screamed and carried on for what seemed like an eternity.

There is nothing more frustrating than being furious with a dead man. I was screaming at the heavens. When I finally regained my composure, I wrote her back and told her that I needed her address so that I could return her money. I explained that my husband hated her and I could not accept her money. I thanked her for her prayers and told her that she needed them more than I did. I told her that I would pray for her and her husband and all of the other families she seeks to destroy. I wrote a check and mailed it back to where it came from.

I have no evidence or reason to believe that their affair continued after they were caught. I actually phoned her husband and let him in on their secret. I found out from her husband that she was quite the liar and manipulator. I really do not know if her sending the check was a sincere expression of sympathy, or her way of rubbing salt in my wound. But it really doesn't matter anymore.

The funeral was absolutely horrible. The church was mobbed. People flew in from all over the world. There were hundreds of people in that church, all thinking that my husband had dropped dead of a heart attack. As I looked around the church I wondered if they all would have attended if they had known the truth. Would there have been quite so many tears? There we stood, my three daughters and I staring at a marble box containing my husband. The man I had given the last eighteen years of my life to, left me without even saying goodbye.

During the funeral Mass, I tried to look back and remember the good times. And there were many. We were married for over seventeen years. I would say that fifteen years were pretty damn good. Not perfect...but damn good. We met at work. I was twenty-four and he was twenty-seven. I liked him immediately although I found him a bit strange and definitely goofy. We quickly became friends and once we started dating we quickly fell in love. Only six months later he asked me to marry him, and we were married eleven months after that.

Our love was passionate but that quickly wore off soon after marriage. I blame that mostly on myself. I always thought sex was a naughty thing to do and after marriage, when it is a "duty", it lost a lot of appeal to me. An issue I should have worked on in therapy a long time ago. I guess deep down I blame myself for his affair too. But I think it was more than that. He was the "safe" choice. I always felt that he loved me just a little bit more than I loved him. He was nerdy and silly but the life of the party. He adored and loved me. If I had known then what I know now, I would have run. Actually, the day I met his family I should have hit the road. But we can talk more about that later. During our successful years we had it all. Our marriage could and did make people jealous. Not only were we good partners in life, we were also good business partners. We owned a few businesses and always made a lot of money. Finances were never an area of trouble or disagreement. We actually rarely disagreed and never fought. I thought this was a good thing, but now I know it was bad. He was passive aggressive. I never knew what was bothering him. Whatever he was holding inside eventually ate away his soul. We had three beautiful daughters. We rarely disagreed about parenting and were always in sync in our parenting style. He definitely had a high opinion of his parenting skills. Our girls were and still are very nice, sweet and well-behaved young ladies. He was brilliant. Successful in all he did. I stayed in the background and kept the books, and helped make strategic business decisions. He was in the front. He was smart, and he knew it. He got involved with an ambitious whore at work that was twelve years younger than him. She was riding his coattails for promotion. It almost worked for her. He thought he fell in love with her. They had a lot in common -- both were narcissists, overly ambitious, liars and drunks.

My insurance guy was the only non-immediate family member at the funeral who knew the truth. He could not have run out of church any faster. My sister made the funeral arrangements. I never met with the priest who conducted the funeral Mass. My sister made the arrangements and even lied to the priest regarding the cause of death. We didn't want anything to slip during the service and we were one hundred percent committed to the lie.

I was still in shock, completely devastated and yet still angry over the affair. There were several people in attendance of the funeral whom had traveled with my husband and his whore, had dinner with them and worked with them. Prior to the funeral I spoke with my husband's boss and told him that I needed a list of the work folks that were going to attend the funeral because there was one person who was not welcome. I had to make sure that the whore didn't attend the funeral. If she had the nerve to send me money, she had the nerve to crash the funeral. Thankfully word had gotten back to her and she knew she was not welcome and did not attend. I held my head up high and didn't say a word during the funeral and the repast, but it was fucking humiliating. I wanted it to get back to her that he had a caring, beautiful wife and a wonderful family who loved him.

I thought his co-workers were suspicious. There were about three gentlemen who worked closely with my husband who offered, "If you ever need anyone to talk to, please give me a call." I wonder if they didn't have something to say or ask me. My lips were sealed. I just smiled and thanked them. But I wanted so bad to call. One gentleman had gone into detail with me about how his last conversation with my husband was a great one. He told me that my husband told him that he had quit drinking and he was exercising and had lost a bunch of weight. This was all true. He hadn't had a drink in months and we were having fun exercising together. Another gentleman had a similar story. He told me how his last phone conversation with my husband was a great conversation. He expressed that he was happy in his new position, and was focusing on his family. I often wonder if these memorable conversations were actually his goodbyes to his close friends.

His best friend gave the eulogy. It was beautiful. I thought his best friend would have been suspicious of the timing of his death since my husband did confide his marriage troubles with him. He never questioned me and never seemed suspicious. During the funeral Mass all I can remember is sitting in the front row with my daughters and my parents and looking at a marble box. When I asked my mother what was in the box, she explained that it was my husband. Chills went up my spine. A wasted life, with so much to live for, was now just ashes in a box. There wasn't a dry eye in the church. It was strange but when Mass ended I was the first person to exit the church with my children. Before exiting the pew, I hesitated; I wanted to take my husband with me. I couldn't just leave him alone on the Altar.

During the repast I got up in front of all of my family, friends, and his co-workers and thanked everyone for coming and said some words about my wonderful husband. All my words were true. He was a wonderful person and he was loved. "My husband is not dead." I explained. "He lives on in our beautiful children."

Chapter Four: His Family

No funeral would be complete without the crazy family and his family takes the cake. If I weren't young and stupid I would have run the moment I met his evil family. Here are the dynamics, his father died when he was seventeen years old. I never met him so I have no opinion. My husband never really said a bad word about his father. I know he missed him and had wished that he were still in his life. Once he told me that he could only remember his father hitting him on one occasion when he was a kid. He remembered sliding across the laminated kitchen floor in his footie pajamas after being whacked. He expressed that his older sisters were not quite as lucky as he was. When his father would return home from a long day at work, his mother would tell his father that the girls were bad and the father would wake them up and beat the crap out of them. The youngest sister, eight years my husband's senior, always seemed to get the beatings the worst. My husband also told me a story that he was bullied at school. He was never dressed as nice as the other children at school and he was never quite as clean. The kids made fun of him. The bullying stopped when his father chased one of the bullies home with a three - foot wrench.

I met his mother and his three sisters. His mother died nine years ago. She died of complications from COPD. She was a nasty, miserable person. We were married for ten years before she died. During those ten years I was invited into her home for dinner on exactly one occasion. She was included in all of our family parties and dinners. To give you an example of how "pleasant" she was, during the baptismal celebration of our oldest daughter, (who was a beautiful baby I must add), in front of the entire party, including my mother, she picked up my baby, looked at her and said, "She is an ugly baby. Just like her father."

What kind of grandmother says that about their grandkid? My husband told me stories about his mother when he was a kid. She always drove around town in a brand-new Cadillac, meanwhile my husband and his sisters wore shoes with holes in them and old used coats and ugly clothes. She was mean and cruel and had no love in her heart. My husband was eight years younger than her youngest daughter and twelve years younger than her oldest. He told me that as a child she would refer to him as a *mistake*, as he got older she even told him that she should have gotten an abortion when she found out that she was pregnant with him. She never bonded with my children and had no love for them. She grew up in the foster system, maybe that had a lot to do with her inability to love.

When she passed away, my husband was told from his sister that he was cut out of his mother's will completely. There was a small annuity that the three sisters split, and the condominium was given one hundred percent to the favorite middle daughter. She never explained her rationale to her son as to why he was removed from the will. Until this day we never knew. His drinking became heavier after that day. He came to the realization that his mother never really loved him. Again, I blame myself. I was eight months pregnant when she died and I was too busy with my two toddlers and new born baby to suggest or to insist that my husband go to counseling. She did leave him one item…a gun.

Growing up, he lived in a two-family house. He lived with his mother, father and three sisters. Upstairs lived his paternal grandmother and his step grandfather. The week after his father passed away, his mother kicked the grandmother and step-grandfather out of the house. My husband never saw them again. He had no idea when they died. He didn't have much to say about his grandmother. He didn't seem to have any love for her, but he absolutely hated his step-grandfather. He didn't talk about him much but when he did, it was clear that he hated the man. I often wonder why he hated him so much.

His oldest sister did not attend my husband's funeral. They were estranged. I am not really sure why. I knew there were issues between his middle sister and the oldest sister but I really do not know what happened between my husband and his oldest sister. The only tidbits I received were that when he was a kid he alluded that his sister was inappropriate with him. Showing him her breasts. He never went into more detail than that. All I know is that a month prior to his death I was watching the movie "Flowers in the Attic". A book made into a movie that touches on the subject of incest. He refused to watch it with me and avoided the room. I only met her once, at their mother's funeral. On another occasion, he mentioned that she gave him dirty water to drink, as a result he was sick for several days. Although I had never met her, I was told that she was *evil*. They referred to her as *the beast*. In all honestly, next to his mother, she was the ugliest person I had ever met. If I had met her prior to getting married, I would have run. I never would have taken the risk of my future offspring being as ugly as this woman.

His youngest sister…crazy is an understatement. There was a point in our marriage several years ago that she was put in a mental institution for seventy-two-hour observation over an apparent suicide attempt. Her first-cousin slash boyfriend was a scary dude. One day my husband and I were throwing some sort of family party and she attended sporting a black eye. When asked what happened she told everyone that her cat did it. Seriously? Sitting at the table with my husband, his middle sister and mother I said, "You guys realize that the cat didn't give her a black eye, right?"

They all looked at me, and his mother said "Yeah".

No one did a damn thing. His family just didn't care about each other. It was very strange.

The middle sister and I never saw eye to eye, but she would be considered the *normal* one of the family and his favorite sister. We tolerated each other because she and my husband were the closest. At the time my husband died we were in a petty disagreement. She has chronic leukemia. The day I found out, I immediately wrote her an email and invited her to stay with us for a while. Unfortunately, she took me up on my invitation and proceeded to cause family trouble the entire visit. My husband never had the courage to stand up to his sister or his mother on my behalf. They never made me feel comfortable and I was never welcomed as part of their fucked-up family. They were both nasty narcissists, controlling and manipulative. They often reinvented history and changed stories to fit their agenda. If her leukemia turns deadly, he would have been a potential bone marrow donor. His suicide could potentially kill her too if she is unable to find another donor.

When my husband died I never heard from the oldest sister. The youngest sister attended the funeral. Her parting words to me were, "Well, it was nice knowing you."

His favorite sister never offered to help me or even checked on my kids after his death. I have not spoken to her since the funeral. Keeping the true cause of my husband's death is my gift to her. No matter how terrible she treated me, she doesn't deserve the pain that would come with knowing the truth. Because I always have to have the last word, I wrote a letter to my husband's favorite sister explaining my feelings.

Hello. I hope you and your family are doing well and that your health is good. Obviously my family is going through great change. I have a contract on my house and we hope to move to a small condo soon. Another baby step in trying to start fresh. After several months of therapy, I thought it was time to write you this letter and get my feelings off of my chest. Let me first begin by apologizing. It is my understanding that you learned of your brother's death by a short phone call by my father, with the message not to call the home and we will be in touch. I hope you have come to realize that the entire family was in complete shock. I did not make any phone calls. My sister and parents made all of the funeral arrangements and my parents paid for everything. So if you thought we were trying to be insensitive to you, we were not. Everyone was in complete and total shock. I hope you now understand that.

With that said, I can honestly say that I think my husband would be totally disappointed and disgusted to know that you did not even pick up the phone to see how the kids were doing in the following weeks and months. I had perfect strangers offer me more help and compassion than you. There were so many different ways you could have helped us. My daughters are very smart and they know who was there for us and who was not. I know you spoke to his best friend and conveyed the feeling that you hadn't heard from me. Please know that with all I am dealing with (for example being there for my three daughters who no longer have a father), contacting you was never on my list of things to do. I know you always expected your brother to reach out and contact you and you rarely contacted him, but I do not feel the same way. Life has been turned completely upside down and we all could have used the love of our family.

  Before his death he reached out to you to meet and bury the hatchet and repair relations between our families. You never even followed up with a telephone call. Please know that your family's practice of gas lighting does not work with me.

He and I always extended ourselves to you and your family. Please think back to all of the functions you attended at your home. You (and your mother) never made me feel welcome as a part of my husband's family. My parents welcomed him and treated him like a son. It always puzzled him and I to how you could remain close friends with his ex-girlfriend, who cheated on him, got pregnant by a married man and was very cruel to him, but you never accepted me. I am far from perfect but I always loved him. I always tried to be a good wife, mother, and I sacrificed and supported his career one hundred percent. We could never understand why you and your mom were never happy for us.

Since I keep mentioning your mother, I think I owe you some explanation. He and I often joked about the "tale of two moms". We would refer to her as "my husband's sister's mother." When your mother died, he was faced with the perceived reality that his mother never loved him. His drinking increased significantly after she died. He never really dealt with it or got over it.

He was very secretive about his past. I know he was emotionally abused as a child, but I always suspected there was more than he ever told me. If you ever want to enlighten me, I would really like to fill in the gaps. There was a side to him that was a stranger to me.

We (now I) do not talk about your mom to my kids. I will never lie to them and say that she loved them or that she was a kind and loving person, because she was not. She did not love him or our children. She made that clear upon her death. Too bad she didn't have the courage to tell her son during her life.

I think your younger sister summed up your family's compassion and love for us when she said, "it was nice knowing you", to me at my husband's funeral.
-Your sister-in-law

My daughters and I are so very blessed because we have a wonderful loving family. My parents give love to my children equivalent to the love of over one hundred grandparents. I don't know how I would have been able to get through the days, weeks, and months after my husband's death without the love and support of my parents and my sister. I always took the love of my family for granted until that awful day. I think one of many reasons why I would never seriously consider committing suicide is because if the deep unconditional love I have from my family. My husband was not as fortunate as me.

Chapter 5 – Why?

The day after the funeral I heard a little voice. "Mommy", said my eight-year-old, "What about the money? Daddy had a job and went to work. How are we going to buy food?"

I looked at her and smiled, "Oh baby, Mommy is an educated woman. I can always work. We will never go hungry. I promise." I tried to exude confidence. But I was terrified. I hadn't had a real job for thirteen years. We had insurance but there are suicide clauses on insurance. I didn't know if I would get paid on it because my husband committed suicide. I doubt he thought enough about us to check. My anger started to grow. How could he do this to us?

The funeral was over. The Facebook chatter had stopped, my friends and family had gotten back to their lives, and there I sat in an empty house. My husband was dead, my kids were at school, and even my dog was dead. I was alone. Nothing else to do but to think… WHY? I thought I had said something awful that drove him to do it. I know I had said some terrible things. I was furious. But I was starting to realize that it didn't make sense. Yes, I was pissed about the affair and he was wrong. But the punishment didn't fit the crime. He certainly didn't deserve to die just because he decided to sleep with another woman. If all people who committed adultery killed themselves, there would be very few humans left on this planet. I had to be missing something. All day, every day for the next several months, I spent digging through his computer and all of his personal belongings. I needed answers. Who was this person?

I was able to tear through his computer because three months prior to his death he wrote all of his computer passwords in a notebook. Strange, because with the exception of that notebook there were no other passwords written down. He also had passwords saved in his Evernote account, but that Evernote file was also referenced in his hand-written note two months prior to his death. It was like he was expecting me to be looking for it. Without these passwords I would have been technologically paralyzed. He was in charge of all the technology in our household. Without the passwords I would not have been able to administer my email accounts, our cell phone accounts, his stock investment account, frequent flier miles, even our home thermostat. In seventeen years of marriage he never wrote down his passwords, why now? Then it clicked; he had been planning his death for months.

I looked at every electronic file on his computer. I even looked at deleted files. I didn't find much, it was wiped clean, but what I did find was interesting. Two months prior to his death, our oldest daughter received several academic and leadership awards. She worked extremely hard that year in school and deserved every award she earned. He was in town and attended the awards ceremony. At the end of the ceremony I told him that I felt like I deserved some of the awards too since I helped her along the way. I could tell he felt guilty because he knew that while I was home helping our daughter, he was out screwing his mistress. I was glad he felt guilty. When looking through his computer I found a deleted Evernote from that day, as I cross-referenced it on my calendar. It was a link to a helium company. If you spend time on the Internet you will notice that sick people post ways to kill one's self. Putting a plastic bag over your head and inhaling helium is becoming quite popular. I can assure you that there were no parties being planned at my house during that time period. There was no other reason to be researching helium delivery companies.

That deleted Evernote was my second clue that he had been planning his death. Unlike the day he died, I was in a great mood. Our family had just gotten off an awesome weekend getaway together, I wasn't fighting with him over the affair, and I was elated and proud of our daughter. I was not in a bad mood. Why was he researching helium on that joyous day?

I spent my days alone, crying and screaming all day. I was filled with sorrow, despair, guilt, anger and helplessness. The guilt was overwhelming and my depression was paralyzing. The only socializing I did was with my therapist, as I was visiting him four times a week. My therapist tried to tell me that it wasn't a spontaneous act. There was nothing I said or did that could drive a grown man to kill himself. Whatever was going on with him was in him and I was just a small part on his stage. He tried to convince me that his death wasn't my fault. I remembered the police officer telling my sister that the belt was rigged in the closet for a while. I close my eyes and try to picture his closet before that day. I can see the brown belt hanging from the top self. I don't know if that is my mind filling in the blanks or if the belt was there and I saw it every day. I was becoming convinced that his suicide was not a spontaneous act. He had planned it.

I also found it very strange that most of his passwords had been changed to some form of "Faith in God". We are not an overly religious family. We drag our kids to religious studies but I can't say we are faithful about praying the Rosary or attending church every Sunday. He tolerated church too and did have faith in God but my husband was by no means a religious fanatic. When I noticed the passwords I remembered a conversation I had with him a couple of weeks prior to his death. I was in his office speaking to him, and he pointed to the corner of the room and said, "That is where I pray.".

There was a small mat on the carpet next to his desk. I didn't think much of it. I just thought he was a little strange but I went about my business. I went back and re-read all of the emails he sent me from the day he was caught having the affair to the day he died. I read them from a different perspective. In the email below, I thought he was being dramatic and was thinking of leaving us. I didn't think or at least I didn't admit to myself that he was thinking of suicide. This email exchange was a month and thirteen days prior to his death.

Husband: "It's a funny day...I've been feeling highs and lows.
I feel highs when you write to me...it gives me hope that you'll want to recreate a story with me, and that you're thinking of me. I've gotten a couple things done at work, too.
I am feeling lows because I realize I don't deserve you and the girls for my behavior over that terrible time. I took you all for granted and I feel I'll never deserve you and the girls. I've been

praying to God for a sign that everything will be ok, and each time I hit a low I've gotten a text from you.

I want to be with you and make it up to you. That entails not lying and sticking by you and the girls. I want to do that more than anything. I am also aware of the huge hole I've dug, and that actions have consequences.

I love you, and I realize that what's best for you and the kids may not be me, given what I've done. And I can hardly bear the thought, even though it's the real truth.

My response: "I am sorry and disappointed to hear that you think me and the girls would be better without you."

His response: "I don't think it...I'm afraid of it being true. I want to make it up to you and them.

I found this email on his computer after he died to our marriage counselor. It is the only email that shows his shame and thought process. It was written twelve days prior to his death.

Today my wife asked me a direct question about the affair and I answered truthfully, but it was different than what I told her in the past. This time I just remembered something I'd previously forgotten. Now we're in the midst of a down day and after several incredibly high

days. The whiplash is unbearable. I can understand and I have validated her feelings, but I am coming down incredibly hard on myself and with awful, dark thoughts. For example, I feel like I'll never be a good person again, I'm a stain on the planet, and that the world might be a better place without me. How can I bring myself up from these awful moments?
REPLY from Marriage Therapist
I am sorry to hear that you guys were in a down day. I hope that things shifted for the 2 of you. This is something that we should talk about because it is more of a process discussion and practice to find what works for you rather than shooting advice over email. We can do this through an individual session or can do with her whatever you feel comfortable with.
-Thank-you for the opportunity.

I remember the counseling session after that email was written. We all joked about it. She asked him if he was ok and he said yes. She said, "A stain on the planet, you are starting to scare me."

We all laughed and he said that he was fine. When I phoned our marriage counselor after he killed himself, she was absolutely shocked. The first thing she said to me was "What happened?"

Again I felt like it was my fault. I told her, "I don't know, I was in a bad mood."

She was a great marriage counselor and we were making progress. She was not trained to identify suicidal behavior. That email should have been sent to my husband's psychologist. He was better trained to see the red flags. My husband inadvertently hurt her immensely and all she was trying to do was help us. I am sure that when she looks back at the email from him she feels guilt from not taking his cry for help seriously. Just like me, she will have to live with that mistake until the day she dies.

      Three days before he died, after his last therapy session, he went to Barnes and Noble and bought three books. Two were sex books. We were enjoying rediscovering ourselves sexually. The third book was titled <u>Forgiving the Unforgivable</u>. He didn't give me that book. I just happened to notice on his nightstand a couple of days before he died. I picked it up and started reading. Basically, it was about being able to forgive a person who wasn't sorry in an effort to move forward with your own life. For example, a wife forgave a husband who cruelly left her for another woman, a daughter forgave her dead father who had sexually abused her. I asked my husband why he purchased that book. I never recall getting a straight answer. I said to him that the book didn't really apply to us because he was sorry and we were making an effort to move forward. That was not an unforgivable act, an unforgivable act is when one of the parties is not sorry. My husband agreed and we did not discuss any further. After he died I picked up the book and wondered why he purchased it. Had he been planning the suicide and this book was for me? I flipped through every page of the book looking for a note, a highlight, a message, anything. I found nothing. I can only speculate. Or maybe he purchased that book because there was someone in his past that he needed to forgive. <u>Forgiving the Unforgivable</u> will always remain a mystery.

Chapter Six: Suicide Victim

About two months after my husband's death, I attended one suicide survivor's group. It was horrible. One lonely single mother sat in the circle and told me about how her only daughter who suffered from bi-polar disorder jumped in front of a train. Another mother spoke of her son who shot himself in the head over a custodial dispute. A girlfriend spoke of her boyfriend who shot himself in the head in front of her, leaving her alone with a two- year and- ten- month old sons. A sister spoke of her brother who suffered from depression and on the third attempt was successful in hanging himself in his family's garage, leaving a wife and children.

I introduced myself as follows, "My husband hanged himself in the closet with our three children home and I have no fucking idea why."

I only attended one meeting. It felt good to get my story off of my chest however when I told the group that I was hiding the suicide from my family and friends they totally and completely disagreed with me. They tried to pressure me into telling my kids. I felt like I was being ganged up on. The woman whose boyfriend shot himself in the head in front of her told me that her young boys know that their father killed himself and how he did it. I was scared to return to the group fearing that if I ever ran into any of those people on the street they might reveal my secret in an effort to do me a favor. The suicide survivor group theory is that our loved ones did not "commit suicide", they "died by suicide". It is a brain disease. They were sick. I agree that mental illness leads to suicide and my husband was sick. We expect people who are sick to get medical treatment. If you are reading

this book and are having suicide fantasies, you need to put down the book and GET HELP. Unlike a broken leg or stab wound, other people cannot see your wounds. You need to get help for yourself. Just like you would if you were bleeding all over the floor. Often you will hear suicidal people say, "no one understands me."
      The truth is, we don't. If you are seriously thinking about suicide, your brain is not working like the rest of us. It is not that we don't understand you; it is that you don't understand yourself. Your brain is bleeding. Oozing all over the floor. If you were stabbed in the chest or were having severe abdominal pain, you would get help ASAP. These suicidal thoughts are your brain telling you that you need to get help. Don't bleed to death. Make the call for help.
      I think there is a better term than *suicide survivor*. I am not a suicide survivor; my children and me are **suicide victims**. We are the victims to someone else's *suicide success*. When the famous actor Robin Williams killed himself, it was very sad for all of his fans. Everyone wanted to know why. We all felt sorry for ourselves because we would no longer be able to enjoy his wonderful talent. His fans were his *suicide victims*. The reporters never asked, "How could he do this to his wife? How are his children? Did he have grandchildren? How are they? How is the assistant who found his lifeless body? How is the poor bastard who had to cut his stiff, blue lifeless body off of his noose?" All of those people have to live with the horror for the rest of their lives. There is nothing Hollywood glamorous about suicide.

Chapter Seven: Small Acts of Revenge

During the one suicide survivor meeting that I attended, one of the women who lost a daughter spoke about going outside and throwing ice at her house in an effort to get out her frustrations. My act of relief is not quite as classy. I spit in my late husband's closet at almost every opportunity.

My sister often tells me that she couldn't believe that I had the courage to re-enter our home after he killed himself there. Sure, strange shit happened in the house after his death. As other people who lost loved ones in their house will attest to, lights would blink on and off, fans would go on and off, I could feel his presence behind me, I would even sometimes smell him. I explained to my sister, "It is not the dead you have to be scared of…it is the living."

Immediately after my husband passed away there was a high hat in our kitchen that would blink intermittently. I knew it was my husband but I never said a word to anyone. One evening I was talking and having drinks with my parents in the kitchen. The light started blinking again. My father said, "What is up with that light?"

I casually responded, "Just ignore it, it is my husband." Well son of a bitch, the moment the words left my mouth, the light burnt out never to blink again.

I was sitting on the couch one evening alone watching television. My children were upstairs completing their homework. I felt like someone was standing behind me. I turned around to look thinking that my youngest daughter crept up behind me. No one was there. I knew it was my husband. I said to him out loud

"If you can't be with me in life anymore, just go away." And he did.

During the weeks and months following my husband's death I went through the stages of grief. I bargained with God but it didn't work. I was in denial and I was angry. My dreams were evidence of that. Until this day, almost every night, he is in my dreams and he is alive. It is a reoccurring nightmare where I realize that he is not dead. I ask him where has he been and he never tells me. I am angry and I send him away. After all I have been through, if he walked back in through the door, I often wonder if I really would send him away. I fear I might. But it doesn't matter because one day I have to accept and realize that he is not coming back. I just wish I knew why.

I am angry. I don't want to be, but I am. In addition to spitting in the closet where he hanged himself, there are small acts of revenge I do that no one can see but me. I took off my wedding rings and put them in a safe deposit box shortly after his death. When asked why I wasn't wearing them, I explained that I couldn't bare the pain of being reminded of my loss every time I looked down at my hand. I put our family home on the market and I donated all of his clothes shortly after his death with the exception of one sweatshirt my youngest daughter wanted. I donated his prized possessions including his drums. Not only did I put my wedding rings in a safe deposit box, I never wear any jewelry he ever gave me. Sexy undergarments and books we were exploring in an effort to get our marriage back on track, all went in the garbage. I sold all of the furniture we purchased together including our bedroom set. I don't keep any photos of him on display in our home. Not only did I never wear

Secret Suicide

black after the funeral, my clothing got tighter and sexier. I secretly had sex with an old friend only five months after his death. After that revenge fuck, I went home walked into his closet, whispered, "Fuck you mother fucker." and spit the biggest gob I could muster onto the closet floor.

I don't feel like a *real widow*. I am angrier than other widows. Unlike widows and widowers I know, I rarely talk about my late husband. I barely talk about him to my children. I feel like I do not have the right to call myself a "widow". My friend lost his wife to cancer. She was a dear friend of mine. I was there when her beautiful face, body and hair were turned to flesh and bone and he held up the bucket and rubbed her forehead as she puked black stomach bile and cancer cells into the bucket he was holding. He deserves the title of widower. I feel like I am one step below a divorcee. My husband not only had an affair like the majority of divorcees, but he also left me. He left me in the worst possible way.

There is no name for what I am.

Only a handful of people know about my husband's affair. I don't like to talk about it and it is no one's business. Nobody knows that he left me willingly. Like most divorced women I have a very negative outlook on marriage. It is odd, but because my husband passed away, people automatically think he was a saint and we had a perfect marriage. I just want to scream, "Just because he is dead doesn't mean he was perfect!"

I shudder when people say, "Oh your husband would have wanted you to be happy."

Actually, I want to scream, "If my husband wanted me to be happy he wouldn't have hanged himself in the God damned closet."

I am *in the closet.* My parents are mostly concerned with this situation not leaking out to my children. My therapist is paid as I see him. My sister has her own problems, dealing with a divorce and two of her own kids. I do not have anyone to talk to who cares just about me. I have to keep this terrible secret and it is exhausting. On the flip side, I guess if I did have someone to talk to I would probably never shut up about it.

The only person I have ever spoken with who I felt could relate to my situation is my insurance guy. He is an old friend, a true professional, and a good catch. I tried for a couple of years to set him up with my sister. That didn't work out since he recently married--a man. He knows my husband's death was a suicide because I had to share the long-form death certificate, which states cause of death, for his insurance policy. He knows that I am keeping my husband's cause of death a secret. We got to talk and I explained that I was exhausted from living a lie. I have to force a smile on my face and act like I was married to a wonderful man who dropped dead of a heart attack. I avoid my friends and keep to myself. Only he understood. He said that when he was coming to terms with being gay he too avoided his friends and had to live a lie. He understood how exhausting it could be. Lucky for him he was able to come out. I don't have that luxury and plan on keeping this secret until the day I die.

Chapter Eight: Putting the Puzzle Together

Not only did I spend my days looking for a note that did not exist, I started researching psychology and suicide websites. I wanted a diagnosis. I wanted to know what happened to him. Did I miss the signs? Why do grown men commit suicide? Is there a website or a book for women like me, living with the lie and protecting their husbands' legacies? Many people who commit suicide abuse drugs or alcohol, my husband hadn't had a sip to drink in four and a half months. They put their affairs in order. He didn't do that either. I remember cleaning out the garage with my parents after he died. He had a bunch of equipment and tools that I had no idea what to do with. I turned to my mother and said, "I wish he would have cleaned out the garage before he killed himself."

He made future plans. We had plans. The emails I have shared with you showed that we were working on our marriage and planning our future. He never talked about killing himself to me to me. He didn't give away his prized possessions. He didn't say goodbye.

When he was a young man, prior to meeting me, he saw a therapist. He always spoke very highly of the therapist and of his experience in therapy. Knowing that he was not opposed to therapy, I always believed that he would seek therapy again if he thought he needed it. After his suicide, I tried to contact his old therapist in an effort to get some answers. Maybe there was something in those old files that would shed light on why. Of course, luck would have it that his therapist was deceased and I did not receive a return phone call from the therapist that took over the practice. It was another dead end.

One thing that he did do that was very strange was that he talked to himself. He always talking to himself since we met, but it got much worse in the last couple of months prior to his death. It was never audible and I never knew exactly what he was saying. When he was in the bathroom I would hear him mumbling to himself. Shortly before he died, I heard him talking in his office. I thought he was on the phone. Since I was so concerned that he was talking to his whore again, I asked, "Whom were you talking to all day today?"

He answered, "No one. I wasn't on the phone."

"But I heard you." I pressed, "Were you talking to yourself?"

"I must have been," he answered.

I thought it was strange but again, I was used to him talking to himself. I really didn't realize how odd it was until one day after his death I was in family therapy with my three girls and Dr. M. He asked my middle daughter what she remembered most about her dad. Her answer was strange; "Daddy was always on the phone or working or talking to himself. I am not quite sure what he was saying to himself but I used to try to listen and try to figure out what he was saying. But I never could figure it out."

My ten-year-old was intuitive enough to realize that something was off with her father. I wish I had seen it too.

I found a very odd deleted Evernote that he wrote to himself over a year prior to his death but just around the time he allegedly began his affair. The title of the note was *Muse*. The note was so very odd and did not paint a picture of the man I was married to. It reads as follows:

> *Be crisp on what a muse is.*
> *You are my muse. You more rapidly than most understand my thinking, and you can expand or improve on it. So explicit is my trust that I take your feedback and re-incorporate it, thus expanding, refining, and improving those ideas. So explicit is your trust of me that you don't dismiss my intuitions as misinformed or misguided.*
> *This is so powerfully attractive to me. I think deep down I have a sense of loneliness. I see connections and I see things that most people I know don't. I feel a bit like Haley Joel Osment in "The Sixth Sense". I see the ideological version of dead people. Most people don't ever see these otherworld ideas, even when I actually point them out, like a ghostly elephant sitting next to them. You not only see them, but when I share them you're able to help me see them more clearly, and see other things connected that I've missed, so enthralled I am with the elephant. Therefore, I'm not just accompanied, but I have an ally, a trusted partner.*

A muse is a woman who is the source of inspiration for a creative artist. The note is from my husband to his whore, clearly he is a narcissist and is expressing how attracted he is to her and I guess how well they work together. But the note gets really weird. Seeing dead people and invisible elephants? The man I knew did not talk like this. He wasn't strange or overly philosophical. It was almost like this woman brought out another person in him. A person I didn't know and he never showed me. Was he beginning to go mad? Did his whore trigger a correlation with a character in his past? Was the abused boy coming to the surface?

Desperate people do desperate things and I am a desperate woman. I had never done anything quite like this before, but I hired a psychic medium. I was exhausted from searching and I wanted the medium to tell me where the suicide note was. I know this sounds strange, but I wanted an apology from the grave. Unfortunately, I didn't get what I was looking for. The medium knew a few things about me that were interesting but not mind blowing. He knew I gave his car to my sister, he referenced rainbows, he knew about an angel statue that was given to me as a gift after my husband died. My grandmother had an uncommon name and he knew that too. Again, interesting but not really. He also said, "Did your husband have a friend named *H?*"

I answered, "Yes."

He said, "You need to contact him. He has clues relating to your husband's death."

"Ok." I said. My reading was done and I thought to myself, there is no freaking way I am going to call *H*, and tell him that a physic medium told me to contact him because he has clues relating to my husband's death. *H* didn't even know it was a suicide. I chalked it up to a waste of time and money and I forgot about it.

Several months later came H's birthday. I sent him a friendly Facebook happy birthday message.

His response surprised me.

Thanks D. How are you and the girls doing? I'm so glad you have been so strong and taking care of your amazing girls. I miss your husband a lot. He was a dear friend. I had some very special comments sent from colleagues last year, which speak to how much he was loved at work. I wasn't sure if you might want to see them when you are ready. I saved some of them in case.

I didn't know if I should open it with you, but I know what happened to your husband. Due to some very strange luck I ended up talking to a sales guy who covers Panama and lived in your community at our company's Christmas party in December. I guess he knew a neighbor who you know and sadly told me what I suspected with regard to his passing. It certainly weighs on me heavily and I wish I could have somehow intervened better as a friend – and I did try several times, including when I last saw him a few weeks prior to his death. If you ever want to talk privately with me, I'm here, and if not, I completely understand. Sorry to be heavy but I sometimes feel that I owe you some transparency if it could help in some way. Sincerely –H

Oh shit! When I read his note, my jaw dropped and my stomach flipped. I tried so hard to keep this secret and I was terrified that the truth was out. The psychic was right.

We spoke on the phone and he explained that he found out by a very strange coincidence while chatting with a stranger, finding commonalities he realized that this man lived in the same neighborhood as my late husband and me. H told him that my husband lived there too. The man explained, that he didn't know my husband personally but he knew about the suicide. Word of the suicide had spread around our thousand-home neighborhood like wildfire. Allegedly everyone knew. Please know that of this very large community, that enjoyed the gossip, not one family introduced themselves or offered any kind of assistance, support or kindness. H explained that he was shocked and had to hold back his emotions. He had just gotten confirmation of what he had dreaded.

We were on the phone for a couple of minutes before he dropped a bombshell, "I have to ask…did he hang himself with his favorite belt?"

"Yes." I answered, "Why?"

"He told me he would." H continued, "He also told his girlfriend that he was going to kill himself. She told me that he was in a rage during a conversation after their breakup and he threatened that he was going to do it."

Obviously, H was feeling tremendous guilt. "I wish I had said something to you. I thought about calling you but he was my friend and I didn't want to do anything that would hurt our friendship. It wasn't the first time he had talked to me about suicide. I was becoming numb to it. I remember several years ago I ran into him at an airport and he looked at me and said that sometimes he just feels like jumping off of a building. He said that he wondered what it felt like to fly."

H also explained the last time he saw my husband, my husband confided in him about having the affair and getting caught. He told him that he felt really horrible and guilty over the affair. He said he was really sorry, but that if I didn't forgive him and we weren't able to get our marriage back on track, that he was going to hang himself with his favorite belt. H admitted that he laughed it off and said that hanging himself with a belt was a little drastic. They both had a chuckle.

I always feared that my husband was so in love with his whore that maybe he ended his life because they had broken up and couldn't be together. H explained that was not the case. He said that my husband had almost a persecution complex. Meaning that when things weren't going one hundred percent his way that he felt like he was being ganged up on or there was a conspiracy against him. H and my husband worked together for about ten years and knew each other quite well. H said that he had seen this persecution complex peek its head out on several occasions. Most recently he explained that his love for his whore, quickly turned to rage and hate. H was actually fearful that my husband might have actually hurt the woman if he had ever seen her again. H explained that their extra marital affair was mutual and it was odd how he turned on her like a snake just because his wife caught him.

I told H about him talking to himself, researching and planning his death and his strange behavior. I told him that I was beginning to think that he went mad. H agreed. He too felt that my husband went mad.

He explained that he noticed a huge change in him after he got caught. "He was like a jailhouse inmate who found God or a Hare Krishna. He lost his grasp on reality. He made me feel uncomfortable with his holier than thou God speak."

I never even knew he told H of his marital troubles and I certainly didn't know he was becoming a religious fanatic. I was glad to hear that he had someone to talk to. H now lives with the guilt that he should have told me. Maybe he could have been stopped. I tried to put his mind at ease and explained that I probably would have just said that he was getting counseling and he would be fine. I tried to save H and all of his friends of the guilt by not telling them the truth. I found out from him that all of his close-knit work friends suspect it was a suicide. No one has had the courage or finds it appropriate to ask me. The whore is living in the world of unknowns. She thinks it was suicide but doesn't know for sure. She lives with the guilt that he told her in a rage that he was going to do it, but she dismissed him. I guess there is plenty of guilt to go around.

They were very good friends and he too is positive that there was abuse as a kid. Talking to H proved to be very eye opening to me. He described the affair and the drinking as ways to escape the past. He spoke of the loneliness of the past. Taking away the alcohol was like taking away the medicine. The affair was another remedy to ease the pain and had very little to do with me. Much like a heroin addict, I can't put myself in someone's brain who is mentally sick. I don't understand why people are addicted to heroin and I can't understand why my husband killed himself.

I had NO idea that I was living under the ultimatum that I either forgive him or he would kill himself. I know that he just wanted to hear the words *I forgive you*. But I wasn't ready. I was almost there but I was scared that if I told him that I forgave him that he would think I was giving him permission to do it again. I thought I had one year to forgive, he only gave me four and a half months.

H wanted to know what happened that day. What triggered it? I told him that I wasn't sure. I was just in another one of my manic bad moods. He ruined my life and I was pissed. H thinks that something that was said between my husband and I that day, triggered him to lose all hope. He gave up. I think H is right, but what it was that I said, I have no idea. I said a lot of mean shit. This is the reality that I have to live with.

Unlike his conversations with H, my husband never gave me the impression that he was suicidal or considered suicide a solution to any of life's problems. H knew his childhood was messed up. My husband told him that his father was a drunk and it caused problems in the family. I found that strange, because although he implied that his father was a drinker, he never told me that he was a drunk or that it had caused problems. He died of lung cancer when my husband was only seventeen. He always acted like losing his father young was a big loss in his life and I believe it was. He talked about having infrequent dreams where he is having a beer talking with his dad and he says, "Why don't we do this more often?" His dad just smiles and looks away.

He got to have his father in his life until he was seventeen years old. He only allowed his children to have him in their life for eight, ten and twelve years. My husband always said that he would die young like the rest of the men in his family. It was a self-fulfilling prophecy.

We both agreed that when there is such little love between siblings and absolutely no connection, that something seriously must have been wrong in my husband's boyhood house.

I have suffered from depression my entire life. I was on Prozac when I was in my twenties, Zoloft in my thirties, and again now in my forties. When I am depressed I have a difficult time getting out of bed and finding the energy to do anything. On bad days I am even too depressed to get up to take my antidepressant. I sleep all the time.

My husband never suffered from depression and really didn't understand what I was going through all of those years. After he got caught having the affair we think he did go into a deep depression. However, his symptoms were very different from what I was used to. He couldn't sleep, couldn't concentrate and lost a bunch of weight. I didn't pay much attention to the weight loss because I had forced him to quit drinking and we were exercising a lot, enjoying walks and yoga together. He actually took a yoga class with me the day before he died. I really hadn't noticed how much weight he lost until I found him hanging dead in the closet. He looked really small.

My husband wrote this email to me 25 days prior to his death.

I just finished praying to God begging him to bless you. You are so good and so strong. You are helping me while giving the kids a happy childhood. You encourage me to be better while you are radiating beauty outwardly. I love you for your strength and inner beauty and I refuse to rest until we restore our previous happiness. Stick with me-I promise to make it more than worth your while.

My response was sent twenty-three days prior to his death.

Thank you for all of your beautiful letters. Sorry I haven't written back in a while. I am sorry my mood swings are uncontrollable. I have never felt this way before...one day I am really happy and can see a future for us and on other days

I am uncontrollably angry and can't see past the past.

Thankfully today is a good day. I am enjoying our yoga, bike rides, walks, and our time in bed. Thank you for all of your help around the house and your attentiveness. I know you are trying really hard and you are doing great. I want to forgive you, I want to move forward and I want to get that awful person out of my head. I think we made really good progress with the marriage therapist yesterday. I also am glad you are seeing Dr. M on your own. I think your relationship with your mother and sisters has finally caught up to you. I hope you are able to find peace and realize that your family loves you. I love you. I am so sorry that you felt I rejected you. I don't know why I acted the way I did, but it was not because of you. I do not reject you. I hope you see now in so many other ways how I showed you that I loved you. I pray for peace, strength, happiness and forgiveness every day. I am looking forward to the day where my mood swings subside and I have full control of my emotions. Right now that wish seems hopeless. I hope you stick with me. I want to be a better wife and mother.
-D

I really do not know how I would have adjusted to my new life without the help and counseling of my therapist, Dr. M. In the days and weeks following my husband's death I was more concerned with figuring out WHY rather than focusing on my own healing process. Dr. M had met my husband and saw him for maybe three sessions. He helped me put the pieces together but because my husband killed himself we will never know for sure. The doctor diagnosed him as a narcissist. This could be seen in his decision to have the affair and the way he spoke about himself and his importance at work. The doctor explained that being a narcissist did not make him commit suicide. Many of his clients have affairs and do not kill themselves. He was suppressing shame from his past. His family was not only dysfunctional, but also emotionally abusive. The doctor and I suspect that there was most probably some sort of sexual abuse in his past as well. When I suggested that maybe he chose a woman that was the size of a man because he wanted a man, his reaction was violent. The doctor explained that my anger and abusive language was completely normal for a wife who had discovered her husband was having an affair. He felt that maybe his whore reminded him of someone in his past, or brought back memories of a traumatic event that he had suppressed in his memory. It was possible that he really was suffering from PTSD from childhood trauma. The doctor explained that I was simply playing a part on his stage. If this situation didn't kill him, there would have been another event in his life that would have ended in the same result. He was a ticking time bomb. Without getting help, he was bound to explode. Something that awful day triggered him but we will never know what it was. We will never know to whom he was talking. He was depressed, maybe he had a multiple personality disorder, and he probably experienced a psychotic break.

After many months of searching for answers, I realized that I knew all there was to be known. I wrote a letter to my daughters. Below is another excerpt from the letter summarizing what I believe to be the truth.

There was a side of him I never knew and didn't like. I always trusted him when he traveled, I gave up any career for myself to stay home with you kids and help him in his career. We were partners. I always worked for him when we owned businesses, I encouraged him to take risks and I always supported him in his decisions and career opportunities. But then after all I did for him, I felt like he threw me away at the first opportunity. He found a new partner. The basis of their shallow relationship was based on work. They were two narcissists feeding off of their huge egos.

His messed-up childhood contributed to his suicide. That is what I believe and Dr. M believes. He did not do this because he hated me. He certainly did not hate you kids. He loved you very much. He felt he didn't deserve us. He hated himself. As Dr. M and the endless research I have done explain, he felt guilt over the affair. Guilt is a normal reaction. But guilt doesn't drive people to suicide. He had a narcissistic personality. He was selfish and cared about himself – that is why he lied and had the affair- but narcissists don't commit suicide. He was feeling shame. Shame is not "I did a bad thing" like an affair, shame is "I am bad and I shouldn't be here". That shame was developed when he was a child. He had a dark side to him that he kept hidden until it was triggered and took over (the affair). He was emotionally neglected as a child. He told me that once he wasn't "cute" anymore, his family wanted little to do with him. His mother was also a narcissist. She was mean and cruel. She kicked him out of the house when he was only nineteen years old so she could bring a man into the house.

His family never made me feel welcome and I never fit in. Maybe now I think that they would not let me in because they had too much to hide. Did he hate his sister? No, he hated himself and was too selfish to see past his own pain.

When he became successful his mother was never proud of him. She called him "her rat fink son".

The point of giving you all of this background information on his family is to paint the picture that something was not right in his house growing up. I have spoken to Dr. M and the only thing that makes sense is that something terrible happened to him when he was a kid, something that brought great shame. What was it exactly, I am still searching but I doubt I will find it. He didn't want me to know and he took it to his grave. He could have repressed it and not known himself. Could something terrible have happened to him from his step grandfather, father, older sister or someone else? I don't know. I want to know what caused this deep shame that lead to his suicide. I will keep searching.

Was he talking to another personality? The person who lead the double life during his affair? The little boy who was emotionally abused and possibly physically or sexually abused? That was his dark side. Who was the person who hated himself, who didn't say goodbye, who didn't ask for help? You will see in his *emails to me that he was making promises and planning future events. It was like one part of his brain wanted to live but there was another personality who did not want to live. That dark, scared boy won. Maybe that other personality emerged after the guilt of being caught having an affair.*

I pray every day for signs, for knowledge and for understanding. I don't know if I will ever know why he did it or why I was so tired that day that I couldn't find him sooner so I could have saved him. Why didn't God help me save him? I have come to terms with the fact that God let it happen and it's not my place to ask God why. I am not mad at God. Yes, I am very mad at my husband.

I am still angry over the affair. In addition I am angry he left me, left us, didn't ask for help, died, committed suicide, did it during the day when you kids were home, did it at home for me to find him. He did love his family. The person who did those selfish acts is not the person we knew and loved. I can only conclude that he was very sick and we didn't know it. These are the same words I said to you kids the day I had to tell you that your father passed away. He may have had a psychotic break, and/or a multiple personality disorder. Depression, narcissism, shame, all stemming from a tragic event in his past brought out by the current events of his bad choices. I truly believe he was mentally ill. Something happened to him and he changed. Dr. M said that he was a ticking time bomb. He was carrying something terrible from his past around with him and never told anyone about it. An event in his life was eventually going to make his dark side come to the surface. I believe that getting caught and watching the consequences of his actions affect me, hurt him. I did not kick him out, I did not ask for a divorce. I was willing to try to work it out. We will never know, if it wasn't the affair, something else in his life could have eventually brought out this psychotic break/multiple personality or whatever you want to call it because we will never have a true diagnosis because he is gone. Mental health is a mystery in science. I hope by the time you read this letter, mental health will have been studied and better understood.

I didn't want you to think your father didn't love you. He loved the three of you very much. He didn't love himself.

My therapist, priests and suicide professionals think I should tell you the truth, or at least tell you when you are older. The professionals feel that if I tell you the truth now you will not be resentful and mistrusting and angry with me in the future. I see their point but I cannot see any reason to tell my young children that their father died by suicide. I just can't see the benefit. I really can't see the benefit to ever telling you. He will always be just as dead. I pray every day that I have made the right decision. If I have not I hope you find it in your heart to forgive me one day, I was only trying to protect you.

I am trying very hard to forgive him for the affair and for his cruelty of leaving us. I really feel he was very sick and I did not know it. There was darkness in his past that he never shared with me. I am certain that the shame and worthlessness he felt before he died was rooted in his past. We had fifteen good (great) years of marriage. He made the choice to have an affair. He did not feel guilt while he was doing it, but he felt shame after he was caught. Then, his past caught up to him. Those were his choices, not mine. I have terrible feelings of anger *towards him and his family. I am working hard to forgive. I want to have a happy life. I want to raise you girls into the beautiful women that I know you are – successful, independent, caring and kind. It is my goal and my purpose. I live for you. I promise to always try my best to be a good mother. I know I will make mistakes but I promise to do my best, which is what I always ask of you. If you are reading this letter and are angry with me for not telling you the truth about his death, I hope you can put yourself in my shoes and try to understand. Please do not be angry with him. He loved you girls very much. He was very sick and hated himself. If you want to be mad, be mad at whatever it was in his childhood that created such shame and loathing of himself. He couldn't forgive himself for the affair, but it was much more – I don't think that we will ever know.*

    I will never know why my husband committed suicide. He didn't want me to know and he took it to the grave with him. It doesn't matter why. He is gone and no truth will change that. He should have asked for help.

    I thank God every day and night for protecting my children. Our bedroom door was not locked and they could have easily found their father hanging by the neck from a belt in the closet.

    I am a forty-four year old woman and can't sleep at night haunted by the vision of what I found. The kids never saw their father dead, not in the house and I had him cremated. They never saw a thing. I pray they remember him as the happy and loving father he once was.

    What if hit me during a conversation with my father. "D" he said, "It could have been so much worse."

"What do you mean? This is pretty freaking bad Dad." I replied. At first I didn't understand what he meant. But after a moment I understood exactly what my father was trying to say.

My husband was not a violent man. He never raised a hand to my children or I. He rarely even raised his voice. But he snapped. Maybe it was a psychotic break, maybe not. What if he decided to take me out with him? One night we were driving home from dinner. It was a date just between the two of us. There was a barrier in street and he came uncomfortably close to hitting it head-on. I screamed and he swerved out of the way. At the time I thought it was dark and the barrier was ill placed, but what if he thought about taking us both out and changed his mind?

What if he decided to take the entire family? If he had a psychotic break what would have stopped him? His mother owned a gun. It was the only thing he inherited from her after her death. She took him out of her will and him and our children got nothing, with the exception of a gun. Because we have young children I insisted he keep the gun outside of the home. He fought me on it but I won. The gun was kept with his best friend who is a police officer.

One evening while out to dinner with my husband's best friend a few months after his death he turned to me and said, "I have something that belongs to you."

I knew he was referring to the gun. I replied, "I know you have his mom's gun. You can keep it. I don't want that fucking gun. Just make sure that evil bitch didn't kill anyone with it."

His response said it all, "I already did."

I also thank God every night that that gun was not in our house on that terrible day. My father was right, it could have been so much worse.

Chapter Nine: We are not alone

Sitting at dinner with a friend of mine, we discussed the suicide of her ex-husband. Like most people, she believes that my husband died of a heart attack. She shared her story with me.

"My ex-husband purchased a suicide kit over the internet. When I received the call that he was dead, I had no idea what had happened. The only words I could understand was that he was dead and there was a bag over his head. I had no idea what that even meant. His father and mother would not make the trip to identify his body in the morgue. I don't know if it would have helped because there were several days between when he killed himself on Mother's Day in his father's home and when he was found by the poor crazy neighbor. As a result, the state would not release his body for burial and did not accept his driver's license as proper identification. I later found out that he put a bag over his head and inhaled nitrogen. His face turned blue and he was unrecognizable. My dead ex-husband was kept in the morgue for six months. My daughter and his mother had to submit DNA samples. It took six months to get the results back. My ex-husband was no prize but he always paid child support. It was an extremely difficult six months waiting for my daughter's social security to kick in. "

"What did you tell your fourteen-year-old daughter?" I asked. She had no idea why I was fishing for information.

"At first a just told her that he had a heart attack. I suspected it was more but I wasn't sure. She said turned to me and said, at least he didn't commit suicide. "

"Wow," I said. "Why did she assume it was suicide?"

"She had been telling everyone that he was depressed, including his father, her grandfather. She even told me that he needed an intervention, but there was nothing I could do, he was my ex-husband. I was never going to tell her the truth but his asshole parents threatened me."

"What? Why did they threaten you?"

"Well", she continued, "They said that she deserved to know the real reason he died and that she could possibility find out one day on the Internet or someone could slip. They felt that she would have trust issues with me if I didn't tell her the truth. I couldn't take the chance that they wouldn't interject themselves into my relationship with my daughter, so I had to tell her the truth."

"What did she say?" I pressed.

"She wasn't surprised. She knew he was depressed. Personally, I think he finally started taking anti-depressants and they gave him just enough courage to do it."

"You blame it on the anti-depressants?" I asked.

"Yes I do and his fucked-up parents. Clearly, he had mommy issues as he killed himself on Mother's Day in his father's house. His father later admitted to me that they were too hard on him. Then never gave him encouragement and always put him down. They thought it would toughen him up, but they were dead wrong. They wouldn't even pay for his funeral. I had to pay for my ex-husband's funeral so my daughter would be able to put her father to rest. They actually fought over his ashes. In the end my daughter received half of his ashes, his father received a quarter and his mother the other quarter."

"That is horrible." I said. Internally I was thinking I guess I am not alone. There are no happy endings when it comes to suicide. Someone always gets hurt unintentionally. "How are you and your daughter doing now?"

"My daughter is doing well. It was a rough couple of years but she got through it. She still has crying fits and misses her father but she knows he was sick. I must be a really bad person because I am so very angry still. I can't believe he just left me with a kid to raise all on my own. When she gets upset I just want to scream at him."

"I don't think you are a bad person because you are still angry with him." I said softly. All I could think to myself is that if she thinks she is a bad person for being angry with her dead ex-husband, what the hell am I? The anti-Christ?

Then I asked the stupidest question. "Why did he do it?"

"I don't fucking know. I guess he was sick. He was always depressed and drank a lot. But honestly suicide is an epidemic."

"I know," I agreed.

She continued, "Did I ever tell you about the woman I work with? I saw her on Friday at work and she looked fine. She was all smiles and was happy it was the weekend. When she didn't show up for work on Monday we later found out that she shot herself in the head and her teenaged son was home."

"Oh my God, that is horrible." Again, I asked the world's stupidest question, "Why?"

"I don't know." She said. "Her husband blamed it on her stress at work."

I decided to share my feelings with her. "I think it is extra terrible when people commit suicide when they have children. I just will never understand it." I shared someone else's story, "I remember when a man in my town hanged himself in the garage in the middle of the night. He had four kids, all under the age of six including a pair of twins and they were all home."

"Oh my God." Then my friend asked the stupid question. "Why did he do it?"

"Nobody knows. His wife was a friend of mine because our kids played together and she blamed it on his prescription sleep aid that he took that night".

Anti-depressants, sleep aids, messed up childhoods, and work stress, we all want to blame something. Sometimes I blame my husband's messed up family; other times his whore, but mostly myself.

She went on, "My ex left a suicide note for my daughter. I read it the other day and I just thought it was a terrible thing to write. In the note he told her that he knew that she would have a hard time with his death because of her age but basically she would have to understand that nothing else could be done about it." She paused, then spoke, "Really, nothing could be done about it? How about not doing it? That would have helped. Selfish son-of-a-bitch."

My friend continued, "I have not had an easy life. I am divorced, a single mother, I have money troubles, I lost my father, I take care of my sick mother and I have my own health issues. But whenever my life got really bad and it seemed like the pain would never end, life always got better. I never felt like I wanted to end my life. There is always hope in tomorrow. "

She became more animated, "As parents we teach our kids to persevere and to never give up. What kind of message was he sending to his fourteen-year old daughter? That it's ok to give up? That suicide is a solution? It isn't. You'll have to excuse me but I get so angry thinking about it."

"I guess we'll never understand." I stated. Internally I was screaming. *I know how you feel. I am there. It isn't fair. I wish I could talk to you.*

Chapter Ten: The Ripple Effect

Solving the mystery of why my husband committed suicide isn't the purpose of this book. He didn't want me to know. He took it to his grave. Could I tell his sisters the truth and try to guilt them into revealing their family secrets? I guess…but that isn't going to bring him back. I am not close to his sisters but I would never tell them the truth if they didn't ask me for it. It isn't fair to them. No one deserves this pain. Keeping this secret, keeping this pain from them is my gift.

My real name is irrelevant. I could be anyone. I could be the young widow next door, your child's best friend's mother; I could be your best friend. There are more women like me out there.

The reason why my husband committed suicide is also irrelevant. Although the nuances of my story are unique, the theme is the same. Suicide is an epidemic.

As I stated in the introduction I hope to save one life. I am not a mental health professional and I would never judge or minimize the pain of someone thinking about suicide.

My young children frequently ask me if I could have a super power, what would it be. My response has always reminded consistent, "I would be a mind reader."

I could not read my husband's mind. If you are reading this book and having suicidal thoughts, you may think people understand what you are going through, but I promise you they cannot. I am not a doctor, but I can tell you that if you are thinking about suicide, your brain is not working properly. You need to seek help. You are your first line of defense. Asking for help is nothing to be embarrassed or ashamed of.

My husband did not leave a suicide note. I searched everything. I even moved our family out of our large seven-bedroom home and packed up every item and went through every piece of paper alone until that house was empty down to the bare walls and floor. No note. Why didn't he leave a note? Why didn't he say he was sorry? Why didn't he tell me why? I have spent hours contemplating these questions. I think I know the answer. In his mind, he thought I knew why. He didn't think he needed to write a note.

When he died, the ripple effect began. The ripple effect is the pain left in the wake of a suicide. People who commit suicide don't end their pain they simply transfer it to the people who love them the most. Like throwing a stone into a lake, the children are at the center. There is no question that my husband loved his children and his children loved him. There is also no question that my kids lost the most. If you have children, you have an obligation to your children to seek help.

Maybe he thought that we would be better off without him. He was wrong. Thinking that others will be better off without you alive on this planet is a cop out. It is just like saying, "I fucked up, and instead of working hard to make it right, I am just going to give up."

My oldest daughter is the bull's-eye of the ripple effect. She has suffered the most. During the year after her father died, she suffered from depression and anxiety. She struggled sleeping and concentrating in school. It was recommended that she go for neuropsychological and psychosocial evaluations. Our family therapist, Dr. M, and a child neuropsychologist who I had only just met when the testing began administered the tests. The report painted a picture of a very sad thirteen year old. She is a child suffering depression and guilt resulting from the death of her father. She has low self-worth and is *sick of having to smile all the time*. I read the report and wept. As I spoke with the doctors I became extremely upset. "HOW COULD HE DO THIS TO HER? IT ISN'T FAIR. SHE DIDN'T DO ANYTHING WRONG. WHY DOES SHE HAVE TO SUFFER THE MOST?"

My children are different than other kids their age. Their childhoods ended the day their father ended his life. In a way they are much more mature. My oldest daughter came home from school one day and she was angry with her best friend. Her friend had expressed fear that if her father found out that she kissed a boy he would kill her. My oldest daughter was angry. "Mommy, how can she say that she is scared of her father because of something so silly? **People don't know what fear is until they are truly afraid.**"

Pretty profound words coming from a twelve-year-old I thought. I was so engrossed in my own sorrow that I hadn't thought enough about my own children. I still have my father so I do not know what they are experiencing. On that awful day, all they understood is that they were eating bagels and watching a movie with their father and then he was gone forever. My children must have been terrified. I would do anything to take their pain away.

My middle daughter is an artist. She sleeps very little and spends hours alone drawing animated characters. Her drawings are beautiful but her characters are rarely smiling and often crying.

My youngest daughter was spared because of her age. She is extremely attached to me. She fears of being left alone and is terrified that something bad is going to happen to me. In the days and weeks and months following my husband's death, she would listen for me. Wherever I was in the house she was always listening. Whenever she heard me cry, she would instantly be by my side handing me her favorite stuffed animal. She just wanted to see me happy again. She would often ask my mother, "When is Mommy going to be happy again?"

I call it the "one kidney theory". My kids are living their life with only one parent. I am the one kidney that is left. Nothing bad can happy to me because I am all my kids have. I try to be extra careful in how I live my life. I am terrified that I might get sick or something bad might happen to me. Who would take care of my kids? I am the mom, the dad, Santa Claus, The Easter Bunny, tooth fairy, disciplinarian, educator, provider, protector and friend. Who will walk them down the aisle or dance with them at their weddings? My children's children are already down a grandfather.

The holidays are no longer a traditionally happy time in our family. It is a time of the year that we have to deal with and try our best to enjoy. We try our best to be thankful and embrace our friends and family, but it is not the same. The past is gone. How much worse would Christmas really be if my children knew that their Santa killed himself?

My parents and my sister welcomed my husband into our family and always showed him love, respect and generosity. My parents treated him like a son. They loved him like a son. He was their son. When they found out about the affair they were understandably angry and disappointed. When my mother found out, her words to me were "Get yourself a good lawyer."

My entire family was working together to find forgiveness and repair our broken family after the truth of the affair was revealed. My parents and my sister forgave my husband and we were all trying to pick up the pieces.

After my husband died, they too suffered the guilt. They feared they were too hard on him. They wished he would have reached out and asked for help. They would have helped him. My parents lost a son that day and my sister lost the only brother she would ever have. They didn't deserve the guilt and pain.

After his death, my parents had the weight of the world on them. Not only were they concerned about their daughter, but they also had three granddaughters to worry about. My husband was supposed to care for and protect my kids and I. Now that job is reverted back on to my elderly father's shoulders. The ripple effect grows.

A friend of mine rented an extra bedroom to a stranger he had known for only ten days. My friend was devastated when he found the man dead of a suicide in his bathroom. My friend was totally distraught and affected by the gruesome discovery. He couldn't sleep, eat, or basically function for several weeks. His horrible discovery was burnt into his brain. I know how he feels. Unfortunately, I couldn't pick up the phone and tell him he wasn't alone. I understand how helpless he feels. The ripple effect extended to an acquaintance made only ten days prior.

If you are having suicidal fantasies or dark thoughts, please seek help immediately. I also encourage you to make a list of your ripple effect. List all of the people who you will hurt if you commit suicide. Do they all deserve it? Make sure you include all of the people who have given you love and shown you kindness in your life. The ripple effect reaches far and wide. Don't forget to include your children, parents, aunts, uncles, cousins, grandparents, best friends, co-workers, clergy, doctors, teachers, and acquaintances who have shown you kindness. You owe it to them to seek help. How do you want to be remembered? Do you want to be remembered by others as the person who gave up, like my husband did? Or do you want to look yourself in the mirror and know that you fought the demons and won?

No one can read your mind. The choice is up to you. Get help. Life and death is not a PG-13 movie. Finding a dead body is horrible. Finding one that died by its own hand is horrible and unedited. The vision of finding my husband hanging by a noose will haunt me forever. If you are having suicidal fantasies, please know that whomever finds your dead body, will be ruined for life. Maybe one day the nightmares go away.

Chapter Eleven: Dating, working & alcohol

Dating as a suicide widow (*swidow*) is also a struggle. It is an internal struggle because a part of me wants to be happy, wants to be loved and doesn't want to be alone. Given the hell I have been through, that part of me feels like I deserve it. On the other hand, I struggle with the guilt of feeling that I had my chance and I blew it. I didn't stop my husband and now my punishment is to be alone and unloved for the rest of my life. I don't deserve happiness.

People have asked me if I started dating. My answer is pretty consistent "I am a forty-four year old widow with three kids and no job. Who the hell would want to date me?"

"Oh, you are being hard on yourself" my friends would say.

"I'm only being honest. I wouldn't call me." I respond.

Several months after my husband's death, I was talking to the neighbor who was kind and drove me to the hospital and to church and watched my kids that terrible day. He asked me if I had started dating.

"Nah." I answered. "I'm not ready."

"Really?" He said. "Shit, if my wife killed herself, I'd be on a date the next week."

I chuckled. He had a good point.

I also have to navigate other people's judgments. Very few people know that my husband was a cheat and no one knows that he left me willingly in the worst possible way, so there is an expectation that I stay a grieving wife for an acceptable amount of time. What is an acceptable amount of grieving time when you are a widow because of an intentional suicide? Is it less than if it was an unintentional death? There are no unwritten rules for *swidows*.

Unlike my divorced friends, there is no joint custody. I don't get free weekends to go out and date. My kids know every move I make. They know what time I go out and they know what time I come home. When is it ok to tell my daughters I am going out on a date and when is it more appropriate not tell them where I am going and who I am with?

The days of lying in bed with your significant other is over when there are children waiting for you at home. The best we can ask for is a fun night out and get the hell home before the children wake up and start their interrogations!

Flash-forward…my husband has been gone for over a year and I found someone crazy enough to date me. Things are going great and my kids seem to be ok with it…so I think. We are in family therapy and Dr. M. asks me how everything is going. The kids are in the waiting room so I speak freely and honestly, "Great Dr. M., my new "friend" came over for the holiday with his daughter and we had a nice day. My girls were good with it. They even helped me cook and clean up the house. Everything is going great!"

The Dr. is happy for me; I leave his office as he calls in my oldest daughter for a private conversation. I am in the waiting room anticipating my date that night when I hear, "Mom can you come in the office?"

Oh shit, I think. Here we go, just when I think everything is going great.

I sit in the psychologist's office and get my ass handed to me by a fourteen-year-old. I sit there and take it.

"Mommy, you are always out with him. We never know where you are. You get home very late. My sisters and me are very concerned. You shouldn't have invited him over for the holiday. It was the worst holiday ever." She vented.

I was screaming to myself. ARE YOU FUCKING KIDDING ME? YOUR FATHER WAS SLEEPING WITH ANOTHER WOMAN AND I WAS ALIVE. HE IS DEAD AND I STILL HAVE TO COVER HIS ASS AND APOLOGIZE FOR MEETING SOMEONE WHO IS RESPECTFUL OF ME. WHY DOES THIS HAVE TO BE ABOUT YOU? WHY CAN'T YOU JUST BE HAPPY FOR ME? I HAVE A RIGHT TO LIVE MY LIFE TOO. I DIDN'T ASK FOR THIS SHIT. I WAS GOING TO STAY WITH HIM AFTER I CAUGHT HIM CHEATING FOR YOU KIDS. HE IS THE ONE WHO LEFT.

I swallowed hard, took a death cleansing breath, "You are right baby. I have been secretive and I have been coming home very late. I disagree that I am out with him all the time, as we usually see each other on Wednesday nights after you and your sisters are finished with dinner and homework, Saturday nights and an occasional Sunday bonus. If it makes you feel better, what if I check in more frequently with you and tell you my location and give you updates if I am going to be home later? I won't include him in any family events anymore if it makes you uncomfortable. But I have to disagree with you; I think this holiday was much better than last. (Last holiday I spent on the couch crying all day. Funny how quickly they forget.) Let's implement family nights on Friday evenings. It will be just us girls. It will be fun!"

"That would be good." She answered.

"Ok, it's a deal."

My daughter left the room and I looked at my therapist. "What am I supposed to do? Stay home for rest of my life?"

"Your daughters lost their father and they are deathly afraid that something bad will happen to you too. I think it was a good idea that you are going to check in with them more frequently. They are resilient and they are going to have to get used to the fact that you are dating and are starting your own new life."

I was so angry. Not angry with my daughter, she had every right to express herself and every right to be upset. I was angry at the universe. Why is this happening to us? I didn't ask for this.

I'd be lying if I didn't admit that the lie of my husband's heart attack was benefiting me too. For example, I started dating a nice gentleman and he took me out to dinner with friends of his. Dining was very enjoyable, and then the question came. "So…you are awfully young. How did your husband die?"

"Heart attack." I quickly answer. I anticipate the next question, because I know it is coming…

"I am so sorry, that is terrible. Was he sick? Did he know he had a heart condition?"

"Nope." I state. "It was sudden."

"No signs?" they push.

"No, nothing." I shut them down.

I feel a little guilty lying to people that I have only just met. But my lie definitely saves the evening from becoming extremely uncomfortable.

How would the dinner conversation have gone if I answered honestly? *My husband hanged himself in the closet. I have no idea why. My kids and I were home and I found him hanging by the neck. Can you pass me the salt please?*

For obvious reasons, I have trust issues and low self-esteem. But I know in my heart that after what I have been through, with the exception of hurting my children there is nothing anyone could do to hurt me any worse than my late husband. I am Teflon. Although a little numb, I am still human and I know I have the capability to love again.

To all *swidows* and *swidowers*, we deserve and are worthy to be loved. We are not sentenced to a life of loneliness because our spouses chose to leave us in the worst possible way. This wasn't our choice and it isn't our fault.

Finding a job has not been very easy. Although I worked for my husband for several years, it has been about fourteen years since I worked in a corporate environment. A friend of mine knew someone who was hiring for a temporary position. I thought I'd give it a try. Once the hiring manager saw my resume, she would not even give me an interview due to my "lack of corporate experience".

Although I have become accustomed to the feeling of rejection, I just could not help but feel a little resentful. *Really, I thought to myself, you don't think I can handle your piss-ant job. You don't know what I can handle. I don't know you either and I bet you are not competent to walk two steps in my shoes. You can put your stupid job where the sun don't shine.*

I am blessed and grateful to receive Social Security from the Federal government for my daughters and myself. It isn't much, but I am very appreciative. I got a good laugh the day I opened a letter from the Social Security Administration. They asked me for an accounting of the money they send me for the kids. Basically, they wanted to know how much of it I saved. I read the letter about five times and then I did my calculations. Monthly health insurance premiums are thirty-two percent of our monthly Social Security allowance, rent is ninety-three percent of our monthly allowance, and I didn't even get to food, school, car, gas or utilities. Needless to say, the "how much do you save each month" question was filled with goose eggs!

One of the best pieces of advice my therapist, Dr. M gave me was to never drink alone. It was tough, but I took this advice very seriously. Sure, I would call a friend and have a couple of drinks while on the phone, but I never sat alone and drank my problems away. Although very tempting, I found that it was necessary to feel the pain and move through life with a clear head. Numbing the pain only prolongs the healing process because you are going to have to sober up eventually and the problems will still be there and they'll probably be worse.

I would joke around with my parents when we would have a couple of glasses of wine, and they would say, "D, if anyone deserves a drink. It's you!"

Chapter Twelve: Healing

    I know there are many books written to help suicide survivors recover from a suicide of a loved one. In an effort to save you some reading time, I will sum it up. You will recover because you have no choice. My husband left me alone with three children to raise. I choose to be happy. I will not let my life be ruined by a dead man. There is no secret sauce. You just do it.
    There is a part of me that thinks my husband sought out an excellent therapist for me in planning his own death. Dr. M, my therapist has helped me tremendously. When my husband first passed away, I was in shock. I attended therapy sessions three to four times per week. We did individual therapy, group therapy, family therapy, and hypnosis therapy. I know that I could not have moved forward with my life without the healing process of therapy. I know that my husband could have been cured and his life would have been saved if he had committed to therapy.
    Yoga is my outlet. It is what I do for enjoyment. Yoga has brought me healing through proper breathing, movement, and concentration. Even when I felt like my life was totally and completely out of control, I would go to yoga and find control and peace on my mat. To just clear my mind for a few minutes a day is worth the effort. Yoga has changed my life.
    I pray often. I thank God for keeping my children safe. I pray for strength, peace and forgiveness. I am not angry with God for what my husband chose to do.
    Ironically, I appreciate life more now than I did in the past. I don't care about material stuff, but I set my alarm to watch the sunrise. I mark my calendar to view

the full moon, I talk to rainbows, and I appreciate a beautiful red evening sunset. My good days are really good. Good days obviously don't come as often, but when I have a good day, I am so very grateful. A fun evening out with friends, watching a movie with my kids, hanging out with my parents were things I always took for granted. I do not take them for granted anymore. Sure, I have bad days. I pop anti-depressants like they are candy, some days I can't get out of bed, and when plans fall through, my disappointments sting more than they ever did in the past. I don't have the luxury to do anything but live my life, raise my kids and find happiness. I love life, I love my family and I love myself.

If you are a survivor, or *suicide victim*, don't let someone else's death ruin your life. Life is short and you have to live on and find happiness. You will be dead eventually too, we all will be. While you are alive, live. I believe we must have faith that one day will be reunited with our deceased loved ones. Be grateful for all of the people who have given you love and shown you kindness during this difficult time.

My only revenge is to lead a good, happy life. I will get there. At the end of the day, I will be fine. I would have been fine if we stayed married, I would have been fine if we got divorced, and I'll be fine now. Unfortunately, my daughters will never have a father. If you choose, you will be fine too. You can love again and find happiness.

I have an opportunity to reinvent myself and I will not squander this opportunity. I look at life differently. I have three beautiful children, a family who loves me, and wonderful friends. I realized that after almost eighteen years of marriage, all we had was a bunch of stuff. Life is so much more than material items. It is about experiences. After I sold our seven-bedroom home I packed my three daughters up and we moved to a two-bedroom apartment on the beach. They all share a room and we are happy. There is nothing better than waking up and drinking a cup of coffee in the morning watching the sunrise over the ocean. The ocean is a healing place. I told my daughters that this is where we are going to *make lemonade*. We now have an untraditional family and we need to embrace it. Not many kids can grow up on the beach. We need to count our blessings.

Humans make mistakes. We all deserve to be forgiven. There is repentance. I was working on my marriage. So, maybe I couldn't forgive. Life could have gone on.

Now I have to find it in my heart to forgive a dead man. Not an easy thing to do. I have days where I am furious, and other days where I try to understand that he was sick and maybe didn't know what he was doing.

How many times have we thought, *I wish he or she was dead*? Trying to forgive someone who is gone is extremely difficult. There is no one to scream at. I can't sit back and watch Karma do her work. I can't even take revenge in simple petty ways. The only thing I can do is live my life. There is no closure. There is no satisfaction. I can't let a dead man break me. I still haven't forgiven him for the affair. Him being dead is absolutely not payback for the affair. None of his sins were worth his life. I may have never forgiven him for the affair, but I am human too. Only God can give a death sentence. My husband was wrong in what he did to himself. I know I will not be able to fully move forward until I forgive him for what he did to himself, to his kids, to me.

Chapter Thirteen: My Plea

My husband gave up much too soon. He should have been honest with his therapist and he should have faced whatever demons were haunting him. Maybe our marriage would not have worked out. He could have gotten remarried. His kids would have forgiven him. He could have found happiness. He could have learned to love himself. He gave up the opportunity to see his children graduate, walk his daughters down the aisle, enjoy retirement, play with grandchildren, and reach his own goals. He was supposed to protect us. Even in this past terrible year, he missed a lot of good days.

You may think that I don't have the right to tell people to get help because I don't know what they are going through. But I can tell you that I have been there. After I gave birth to my oldest daughter, I had very severe post-partum depression. I couldn't stop crying and I was hearing voices…evil voices. I kept it to myself, until the voices got so loud that I knew I needed to ask for help. One afternoon with my baby in my arms I called my husband. I was hysterical crying, "I can't stop crying. I hear voices. I am scared. I need help."

My husband replied, "I'll be right there." He hung up the phone and what was usually a forty-five minute commute from work was a twenty-minute sprint home. He broke just about every traffic law to get home to me.

He phoned my mother and she was at my doorstep a half hour later with her suitcase. I phoned my doctor and he wrote me a prescription over the phone. I was not left alone for several weeks until the anti-depressants kicked in, my tears dried up and the voices subsided.

It wasn't easy asking for help. I was scared of what people would think of me. Would they think I was a bad person or an incompetent mother? Would they take my baby away from me? The most difficult part was the action of picking up the phone and asking for help. Once the call was made, I got help. My baby and me were safe. I was my first line of defense.

Shortly after my bout with post-partum depression, several well-known Hollywood actresses came out and brought attention to this epidemic. As a result, post-partum depression literature and questionnaires have become a standard part of pregnancy care. Maybe effective mental health questionnaires should become a standard part of getting an annual physical.

To the mental health professionals:

I plead to the mental health profession to study suicide. There is not enough research done on suicide. Just like there are many different types of cancer, there are many different types of suicide. Teenage suicide should be studied differently from adult, from elder suicide. Suicide from inherited mental health disease should be studied differently from suicide from situational mental health disorders. What we call a mid-life crisis in men is becoming a deadly time in many men's lives. Money needs to be spent to bring this issue to the forefront. It is an epidemic.

To people like me:

You are not alone. Its ok to be angry and it is ok to lie. Stop blaming yourself. We are not mind readers. We don't know what people are thinking. I know looking back in hindsight maybe there were signs, but we are only human. Our brains don't work like people who are suicidal. If they were giving signs, it would be difficult for us to pick up on them. Be grateful. You are still here. Your life can get better. Reinvent yourself. Find forgiveness.

To people thinking about suicide:

To adults considering suicide, please think of all the awesome events in your future that you are going to miss. Think of all of the people who love you that you are going to hurt. Think of all of the people who depend on you.

To teenagers who are considering suicide...all I can say to you is that being a teenager sucks. Obviously, being an adult has its ups and downs. Even given what I have been through, I would never trade my life to go back to being a teenager. Stick it out, I promise it gets better...much better. Don't miss the opportunity to fall in love, know unconditional love from your children, take control of your own life, make mistakes and find success. If someone is hurting you, they will just move on to hurt someone else when you are gone. The people you love and love you will never recover. The grief from losing a child to suicide is immeasurable and different from the grief of losing a spouse. I would rather my child murder me than take their own life.

Please close your eyes and think about all of the people you will hurt if you kill yourself. Do those people deserve the guilt, pain, and sadness? Does anyone deserve to have the horror of your dead body burnt into their memory? Do you realize that the people you will hurt are the people who love you the most? You may be mentally sick. The emotional pain might be unbearable. There is help. Maybe you totally and completely fucked up your life. Its ok, you are human. You can be forgiven. You can be healed. Life can be rewritten, death cannot be undone;

If you would like to contact Donna, please find below her current email address...

vellad087@gmail.com

www.ingramcontent.com/pod-product-compliance
Lightning Source LLC
Chambersburg PA
CBHW052059070526
44584CB00017B/2255